POCKET
*F*LY FISHING

POCKET
*F*LY FISHING

CHARLES JARDINE

DK PUBLISHING, INC

A DK PUBLISHING BOOK

First American Edition, 1996

2 4 6 8 10 9 7 5 3 1

Published in the United States by
DK Publishing, Inc.
95 Madison Avenue
New York, New York 10016

Visit us on the World Wide Web at
http://www.dk.com

Produced for DK by
COOLING BROWN, Hampton, England

Library of Congress Cataloging-in-Publication Data
Jardine, Charles.
  Pocket Fly Fishing / by Charles Jardine --
1st American ed.
    p.   cm.
  Includes index.
  ISBN 0-7894-1098-2
  1. Fly fishing--Handbooks, manuals, etc.
  2. Fishes--Handbooks, manuals, etc.
  3. Flies, Artificial--Handbooks, manuals,
  etc. I. Title.
SH456.J37 1996
799.1'2--dc20   96-13243
                                          CIP

COLOR REPRODUCTION BY
COLOURSCAN, SINGAPORE
PRINTED BY
WING KING TONG CO LTD, HONG KONG

CONTENTS

INTRODUCTION

INTRODUCTION

THIS LITTLE VOLUME is intended to inspire you with the enthusiasm and passion I feel for a sport of infinite variety and change. Naturally, it is impossible to cover every aspect of game fishing in a book so small, yet all the basics are here. To help you fully explore the ever-changing environments of streams and lakes, I have detailed the correct rods, lines, and flies, as well as the things that game fish eat, and where you are most likely to find them in the water system. I have also provided some essential bankside information that may help in a difficult situation. The foundations are laid here to enable you to develop, fashioning your own style, knowledge, and expertise.

Goat's Toe
A classic lake wet fly that remains successful for trout, sea trout, and salmon.

I would advise any newcomer, or those who wish to improve, to seek qualified instruction, since skills such as casting and retrieving are far

Brown Trout
Among the most sought-after fish in fly-fishing is the brown trout. It is wary, reclusive, secretive, unpredictable, and beguiling.

Landing the Catch
*The moment of truth, as the hard-earned prize slips over the
rim of your net – a consummation of the correct approach,
cast, rod, reel line, leader, fly, and retrieve.*

easier to learn firsthand. These skills must be developed prior to
starting out on a trip. Remember, you do not need a river full
of trout or salmon to practice. A sizable lawn, pond, or
recreation area is all that it takes.

The presiding elements that permeate our sport are the
camaraderie of fellow fishers, the joy of the countryside, and
the sheer beauty and grace of the quarry. Nurture these. In a
shrinking natural world, pristine rivers, lakes, and their
inhabitants cry out for our support, understanding, and, very
often, protection. Respect your quarry and be mindful of those
who follow. Care for our precious surroundings and take that
litter or nylon home. Oh yes, and go out and enjoy yourself.
Tight lines and screaming reels!

CHARLES JARDINE

The QUARRY

LEARNING ABOUT AND KNOWING your quarry is at the heart of fly-fishing. Understanding the trout's preferences for certain areas, its diet at different times of the day, the effects of wind and weather, especially air and water temperatures, is essential for the well-prepared and successful fly fisher. As you delve deeper into the sport's intricacies you will become immersed in a unique world of infinite change and diversity. To borrow a military axiom: "Time spent on reconnaissance is seldom wasted." Knowing your quarry's lifestyle is vital in the gentle art of fly-fishing.

Show a Little Respect
Catch and release now prevails on many waters. Whatever kind of water you fish, always respect your catch: kill it swiftly or return it with minimal distress for the quarry.

RISE FORMS *and* PRESENTATION

BEING ABLE TO recognize signs of feeding is vital. The secret is to scan the surface prior to casting. Trout give themselves away in many ways, the most obvious being a rise, or surface disturbance. This can vary from a huge water upheaval to subtle sips. A shimmer, breakup of a wave pattern, or tiny crease in the current could mean you have found your quarry. An understanding of the trout's diet and the way food is ingested is also important, as is the ability to spot and respond quickly to the trout's rise after the presentation (that phase of a cast when the line straightens and the fly descends to the water). Be ready to respond to the rise, which is followed by the trout inspecting the fly and either accepting or rejecting it.

KEY STRATEGY

If your dry fly or emerger has been refused, try a smaller version or reduce tippet diameter. Flies trapped in the surface film tend to work better than floating types. Stay alert to rises or trout position – wearing polarized glasses reduces glare and improves your vision when searching for activity underwater.

The Complex Rise
If the trout is ultracautious it will go through the inspection procedure of the simple and compound rise, drifting very far to end up facing downstream before accepting or rejecting your offering.

The Compound Rise
When the trout is uncertain about the food form, it will go through the routine of the simple rise but drift back with the current, only taking the fly when it is sure of its validity. Make sure your fly does not drag.

► **Nebbing/Kiss Rise**
The trout trawls through the surface feeding on spinners, emergers, or casualties of the hatch. This form of rise normally occurs during the soft light of morning and evening and in dull, cloudy weather. Use a fly that sits low in the surface film, such as a suspender, parachute, or no-hackle style.

▼ **The Simple Rise**
Indicated by rings widening across the surface, the shape of the rise can be the key to insect stage and type – a kidney-shaped whorl indicates emergers or spinners; the nose pushing through the surface is a sign of hatched adults.

▲ **The Bulge**
One of the hardest rises to read, this occurs when trout take nymphs subsurface. Watch for a lump in the water, a flattening of a wave, or little waves amid a big one.

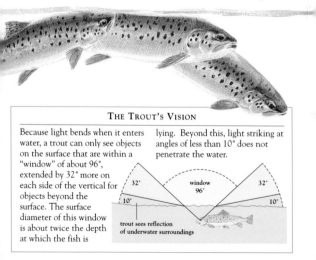

THE TROUT'S VISION

Because light bends when it enters water, a trout can only see objects on the surface that are within a "window" of about 96°, extended by 32° more on each side of the vertical for objects beyond the surface. The surface diameter of this window is about twice the depth at which the fish is lying. Beyond this, light striking at angles of less than 10° does not penetrate the water.

32°   window   32°
              96°

10°   10°

trout sees reflection
of underwater surroundings

BROWN TROUT

THE BROWN TROUT is distributed widely and is considered by many fly fishers to be the ultimate challenge, largely because of its secrecy and unpredictability, which constantly challenge angling methods. It is a lover of rivers and natural stillwaters, and time spent working out its feeding pattern on your chosen water pays off. Time of day is important – in low light the trout will take up station in shallows, margins, and thin water; harsh light tends to drive it into the sanctuary of undercut banks, deep pools, and deeper areas in lakes. In particular, look out for brown trout around obstructions such as old tree roots and fence lines.

AVERAGE SIZE

In food-rich waters, such as spring creeks, the average length of a three-year-old brown trout is 12–14 in (30–36 cm). In the more acidic waters of freestone streams it may only attain 6–8 in (15–20 cm).

▼ **Brown Trout**
Brown trout are easily distinguished from rainbow trout by their lack of spots on the tail fin and pronounced spots, which are sometimes red, on the body.

TIPS FOR CATCHING BROWN TROUT
This species shows a preference for drab, insect-oriented patterns. If in doubt, it is wise to use smaller rather than bigger flies and pay attention to presentation, using as fine a leader as possible.

▲ Brown Trout in Lakes
Its color can vary from bright silver to bronze and buttercup yellow. A lover of cool water, it can be found feeding near the surface in overcast conditions, holding deep when the sun comes out and the temperature rises.

◄ Montana Brown
This trout shows how well the fish transplants and prospers, offering stupendous sport all over the globe.

FAVORITE FLIES

IRISH MALLARD
& CLARET

Spring Creek
see pp. 62–65
Sawyer's Pheasant Tail
Duck's Dun
Beacon Beige

Freestone Stream
see pp. 72–75
Parachute Hare's Ear

Stillwater
see pp. 84–89
Irish Mallard
& Claret
Black Pennell
Minky

Spots on flank can be vivid red in some brown trout

RAINBOW TROUT

THE RAINBOW CAN be caught almost anywhere in the world and in virtually any type of water, be it stream or lake. From its origins in the rivers of the Bering Strait in the Arctic Circle and from Russia down the western coast of the US, this fast-growing species has found favor with anglers due to its fighting qualities, broad-based diet, and willingness to feed in a wide range of air and water temperatures.

▲ Prior to Release
This three-year-old shows not only the beauty of the fish, but also its astonishing growth potential and the silvery bloom of health in its tail.

Heavily spotted tail is a distinguishing characteristic of rainbow over brown trout

▲ America's Finest
The body is silvery and usually has a carmine stripe along its lateral line. The back is usually olive through grayish tan and the fins are sprinkled with small black spots, as are the flanks.

FAVORITE FLIES

PARACHUTE
ROYAL WULFF

Spring Creek
see pp. 62–65
Transition Dun
Duck's Dun

Freestone Stream
see pp. 72–75
Parachute Royal
Wulff
Bead Head Prince
Ethafoam Beetle

Stillwater
see pp. 84–89
Green Butt Tadpole
Distressed Damsel

▲ **Feeding Rainbow**
The rainbow's speed is legendary. Anglers should be careful not to miss the "take" and, during the retrieve, to react quickly when the fish hits the fly at a speed that may break the leader. Generally eager to surface-feed, this fish has just seized a fly fisher's floating imitation.

TIPS FOR CATCHING RAINBOW TROUT

Because of its widespread location, almost all methods will work for rainbows. On catch-and-release waters they can become fussy, which calls for fine tippets, good presentation, and hatch-matching flies. The surface and immediately below are its preferred hunting grounds.

AVERAGE SIZE

A three-season rainbow can reach 7–12 in (18–30 cm), growing to 20 in (50 cm) in food-rich waters.

BROOK TROUT
and CUTTHROAT

BOTH OF THESE SPECIES are native North Americans. The brook – really a char as opposed to a true trout – includes both seafaring and purely freshwater types, and has also found a niche in other countries where suitable cold-water conditions exist.

The cutthroat, on the other hand, has tended to stay in its home waters, often breeding with native rainbows to create a sporting hybrid, the cut-bow. Though found on rivers, this species can attain great weights in the various western lakes, especially Henry's Lake on the Idaho/Montana border and the current record-holding venue of Flaming Gorge Reservoir in Utah. The Yellowstone variety has fewer but larger spots over a deep golden background; the Snake River version has tiny spots over a more somber gold.

AVERAGE SIZES

Brook trout and cutthroat can vary dramatically in size, depending upon the available food source. Both tend to be largest at their seagoing stage, although lake-dwelling fish can also grow very large. Expect both species to be anywhere between 8–20 in (20–50 cm).

Characteristic red spots

▲ **A Perfect Cutthroat Specimen**
This is a fine example of the Yellowstone variety. Where catch and release is practiced, the "cuttie" can become as selective as any other species, calling for hatch-matching artificials fished on thin tippets with delicate and accurate casting.

TIPS FOR BROOK TROUT AND CUTTHROAT
Styles of fishing vary between these species. On balance, a more river-imitative strategy will work for cutthroats. Streamers fished in secluded areas work well for brook trout, especially on lakes where a marabou-based damsel or bugger fished in deep areas can be particularly effective.

FAVORITE FLIES

for Brook Trout

WOOLLY BUGGER

for Cutthroat

TRANSITION DUN

◄ **Brook Trout**
This example of a male in its breeding attire shows just how spectacularly colorful they are. The elongated mouth is typical of this stage, as is an aggressive nature.

No spots
on tail

GRAYLING *and* WHITEFISH

HISTORICALLY REGARDED as "also-rans," these ancient species, especially the grayling, are becoming a cult throughout Europe and America – notably in Alaska where the Arctic grayling is revered. The whitefish is still low on the angler's shopping list. Nevertheless, it has brightened up many a gloomy day of little trout activity.

Grayling are an "alternative" game fish, coming into season, and best fished for, in the autumn and during warm winter days, although mid- to late summer is a favored time in many parts of Europe. Both eagerly take the dry fly, but sunk nymphs offer the greatest opportunity for a fine catch. Smoked grayling makes good eating.

AVERAGE SIZES

Both species vary dramatically depending on location and habitat. On the fast-flowing rivers of Montana it is not unusual to catch whitefish to 3 lb (1.4 kg). Grayling tend to average less than 1 lb (0.45 kg), but on some European rivers they average 2–3 lb (0.9–1.4 kg).

Large dorsal becomes very colorful at spawning times and in Arctic species ——

▶ **Grayling**
Known as "the lady of the stream," grayling are silvery, washed with pale purple and sprinkled with tiny black spots. The jaw suggests it feeds below rather than at the surface.

▲ Mountain Whitefish

Enjoying fairly fast flows, this species, like the grayling, is a shoal fish – find one and you will tend to catch several. Very large scales cover an olive shading to its silver body.

FISHING TIPS

North Country "spider" patterns are used to great effect. Both species respond to dead-drifted gold bead-head nymphs. They will take dry flies with a little color, such as red.

FAVORITE FLIES

for Whitefish

GOLD HEAD PUPA

for Grayling

KLINKHAMMER SPECIAL

Large, silvery scales resemble body armor

SEA TROUT *and* STEELHEAD

B OTH OF THESE FISH represent opposite ends of the spectrum for their species. The sea trout favours the European seaboards, whilst the steelhead can be found an ocean away on the North American west coast. Each can be taken on a variety of methods, but fly-fishing is considered the art form.

Sea trout tends to run during the summer months, peaking in the long days of June, July, and August, although small 'pods' of fish can journey into rivers at any time. Steelhead enjoys a protracted season, 'running' rivers during spring, summer, autumn, and winter.

▼ Sea Trout
Also referred to as finnock, peal, or sewin, the sea trout tends to feed in estuaries near the river of its origin. It feeds on a variety of creatures including crabs, sand eels, and small fish. Though caught along the coastline, it is as the fish returns to the river under the cloak of darkness that anglers are offered the best opportunities. Caution, quiet, stealth, and an intimate knowledge of your intended fishing area are the secrets to fishing for sea trout.

AVERAGE SIZES
Although sea trout can grow to some 20 kg (44 lb) it is more likely for them to weigh 0.9–3 kg (2–7 lb). The bigger sea trout tend to be more solitary. Steelhead are generally larger, with fish entering a river at 5–15 kg (11–33 lb).

FAVORITE FLIES

for Sea Trout

MEDICINE

for Steelhead

TEENY NYMPH

FISHING TIPS

Concentrating your efforts during the hours of darkness will be more productive for sea trout. Fishing pools for both species – especially during low water – can be effective. Always try to observe your quarry prior to fishing.

▲ **Steelhead**
Though vastly different from the sea trout in color and origin, similarities do exist. Both tend to run in groups and take up similar lies, such as heads and tails of pools, overhung shadow areas during intense light, and current-deflecting obstacles.

SALMON

TWO OCEANS GIVE us two distinct salmon types. The Pacific species – the chinook, chum, coho, pink, and sockeye – tend to return only once to the rivers of their birth before they spawn and die. These amazing fish graze the oceans' riches, entering fresh water as bars of silver and within hours starting to change into their vivid breeding colors. From China to the salmon-rich waters of Alaska, Canada, and the northwestern US seaboard, the rivers reverberate with the sheer weight of spawning salmon.

In contrast, the Atlantic salmon make repeated spawning journeys. For their sheer majesty and fickle unpredictability, be it on the great rivers of Canada's lower eastern seaboard, Russia, Scandinavia, or Britain, they remain the ultimate prize.

AVERAGE SIZE

Pacific salmon:
Chinook 30 lb (13.5 kg)
Coho 10 lb (4.5 kg)
Pink 5 lb (2 kg)
Sockeye 7 lb (3 kg)
Chum 8 lb (3.5 kg)
Atlantic salmon:
Grilse 3–6 lb
(1.4–3.5 kg)
Springers and Maidens
8–28 lb (3.5–13 kg)
Adult salmon
44–88 lb (20–40 kg)

TIPS FOR CATCHING SALMON

It is always wise to seek local knowledge. Timing your fishing with that of a "run" of salmon is a critical business, as is matching your rod to the water being fished. Water and air temperatures are also vital factors in deciding fly depth and size, especially where Atlantic salmon are concerned.

▶ **Pink Salmon**
Although the most prolific, pink salmon are the smallest of the Pacific species, tending to run the rivers in the autumn in huge numbers.

FAVORITE FLIES

EGG FLY

FLASH FLY

▲ **Silver Salmon**
*Probably better known as the coho, the silver
salmon runs the rivers from July onward and
keeps fairly close to the surface. Popular flies tend to
be red and white or have blue in their dressing with the
added allure of silver.*

◀ **Humpback Salmon**
*The smallest of the
Pacific species, this pink
salmon is bright silver
with black blotches when
fresh from the sea. Males
develop the distinctive
humped appearance
when it is time to spawn.*

Long-tailed sealice
indicate recent
journey from sea

FOOD *and* FLY
PATTERNS

IMITATING THE FOODSTUFFS of the quarry is the very
heart of fly-fishing. The ability to match the insect with
an artificial fly is the aim. In the case of migratory game
fish, little if any feeding may take place in fresh water;
here the fisher can appeal to the fish's predatory, aggressive
instincts by using a bright lure or triggering a response
with a fly reminiscent of its diet when growing in the river
system. You need to understand the quarry's diet, which
requires taking time in reconnaissance, being constantly
watchful for insects and feeding signs, keeping an
inquiring mind, plus that most potent weapon
of all, *confidence*.

Sifting for Clues
*A net made from two broom handles and a stapled length of net
curtaining is pushed along the river-bed, or through weed beds; the most
prevalent captive insects may then be matched for size and color.*

MAYFLIES

BAETID NYMPH

OF ALL THE FOODSTUFFS imitated by
fly fishers, upwinged mayflies are
perhaps the most loved. They start life as eggs that, after
several weeks, change into fledgling nymphs. They then
attain maturity over the next 12 months.

When the dun (subimago) finally emerges, there is little
to differentiate between species except size. Some sport
different-colored bodies and wings; some species have two
tails, others three. Overall they resemble small yachts.
Within 12 to 20 hours the imperfect fly will have
miraculously changed into the imago, or perfect fly (the
"spinner"), and at this
stage it will mate.

The female then
flies to the water she
has selected for laying
her eggs and, within the
day, dies. This final
stage is referred to as
the "spent" fly and is
relished by the trout.

◀ Stone Clinger
*This typical stone clinger nymph
(Heptagenia, Ecdyonurus, and
Rhithrogena spp.) shows how
perfectly adapted they are for
fast-flowing streams. Your
nymph should echo the flattened
shape and mimic its posture.*

DUCK'S DUN

▲ Agile Darter
This nymph is typical of the large Baetid order. Use streamline nymphs in various drab tones to imitate the various species found in most water types.

▼ A Typical Mayfly Dun
The subimago stage is perfectly shown here in this freshly emerged dun cloaked in drab grays and olives. Use a suitably colored imitation, matching both size and tone. Importantly, fish your imitation "drag free" in a similar manner to the natural on the water.

▲ A Typical Mayfly Spinner
The final stage or imago is the most colorful; the changed clothes from drab to bright should be echoed in fly design. Make sure when imitating the "spent" stage that your pattern fishes low in the surface film.

CADDIS FLIES

GRANNOM PUPA

THIS WIDESPREAD, MOTH-LIKE insect is equally at home on still or flowing water and is an important part of the trout and grayling's diet all year round.

While species such as *Rhyacophila* and *Hydropsyche* live freely, many larvae build an outer protective case from tiny stones, gravel, twigs, and other detritus, where pupation occurs. When the pupa emerges it becomes a vital aspect of diet and imitation. The natural often moves through the water layers in a decided rise and fall, zigzag movement that should be echoed in your retrieve.

Hatching tends to take place in open water from afternoon onwards; very often trout reaction to the adult fly can be explosive as they run for cover along the surface. But be careful – often these violent rise forms result from trout chasing pupae through the layers, momentum carrying them sufacewards.

◀ **The Cased Caddis**
This typical example of the larva in its constructed home is best imitated by a Stick Fly or long shank Hare's Ear, weighted to fish near the bottom and allowed to dead-drift or retrieved slowly.

REALISTIC CADDIS

▲ **Great Red Caddis Pupa**
*The quite tubby, hunched
appearance and well-defined
legs are common to most
types. Common colors
include cream, amber, tan,
shades of brown,
and green.*

▲ **Adult Caddis**
*This caddis (Pycnopsyche
guttifer) occurs in
American eastern and
midwestern woodland
streams. The female can
dive underwater when
laying eggs, increasing its
usefulness to fly fishers.*

▶ **Gray Caddis**
*Caddis fold their wings
like a tent over their
bodies when at rest.
Adult caddis either
feed on flowers
or do not feed
at all.*

▲ **Longhorn Caddis**
*North American species of Oecetis live on stony bottoms
of still and slow-moving waters. Trout go after all stages
during mornings and afternoons.*

FLAT-WINGED FLIES

TUBE BUZZER

O F ALL THE MEMBERS of the vast order *Diptera* – which also includes house flies, bluebottles, drones, crane flies, smuts, gnats, and mosquitoes – the nonbiting midges or *Chironomids* are universally the most available to both fish and fisher. Be it winter or summer, Argentina, Montana, or Hampshire, river or lake, a midge of some description will be active. It is a vital fly for the fisher to imitate, whether in its larval form (often referred to as a bloodworm), the resultant pupa, the emergent adult, or the resting full-winged adult.

The pupal stage is the most useful to the fly fisher, then the adult, which as a dry-fly pattern has brought about a rebirth of topwater fishing on reservoirs. Midge larvae thrive in low oxygen levels, making stillwaters and slow-moving rivers particularly attractive to them.

▶ **Bloodworms and Phantom Larvae**
The bloodworm's color is created by hemoglobin, a substance that enables it to function at great depths. Though difficult to imitate, the constant wriggling movements of the bloodworm make it a prime target for trout. The phantom larva, Chaoborus sp. (inset right), tends to rise and fall in a much more sedentary mode.

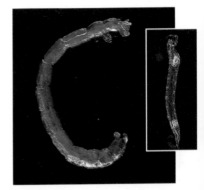

▲ Emerging Midge
The surface film, especially on calm, very humid days, offers the midge a huge barrier to break through. Trout know this and feed appropriately. Use either a suspender or a semidry or lightweight nymph that will hold in the surface film.

▲ Midge Pupa
This curved aspect of the pupa is typical of its lashing movements as it propels itself surfaceward to hatch – echoing this posture in fly design is no bad thing, nor indeed, is the abdominal color breakup.

◄ Adult Midge
Midges occur on many waters throughout North America. Hatches can sometimes be very dense. One of the first major hatches of the season, this fly has the ability to encourage large numbers of good-sized trout to feed in often hostile weather.

PARA MIDGE

STONEFLIES *and* DAMSELFLIES

THESE TWO ORDERS of insects represent opposite ends of the fly-fishing spectrum. Stoneflies inhabit boisterous freestone rivers (though some occur on high-lying acidic lakes, along the windward shore), whereas damselflies and dragonflies, primarily lake fisher's baits, inhabit the slower-moving stretches of rivers.

WOVEN STONEFLY

Both orders follow the egg-nymph-adult cycle. The stonefly nymph (*Plecoptera sp.*) can, in some species, attain a size of 2 in (4 cm) and go through a number of instars (changes of outer skin), creating an albino form. Because the nymph dwells among the stones and boulders of well-oxygenated rivers, fishing an artificial along the bottom can yield results.

The large insects of the *Odonata* order also go through the

egg-nymph-adult cycle. It is generally the nymph rather than the adult that is important for the fly fisher to imitate, and it should be represented in the angler's range of imitations.

The slender damsel is considered the more important of the two to the stillwater fly fisher.

◄ **Small Stonefly Nymph**
More of a mouthful than the damselfly nymph, the stonefly nymph has a sturdy body, two tails, and long antennae.

► **Large Adult Stonefly**
This large, dark adult (Perlodes microcephala) is similar to the American salmon fly.

◄ **Damsel Nymph**
These range from light green to dark brown. Streamlined, with three spiky tails, they are fast swimmers. Their undulating movement attracts trout.

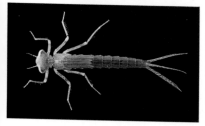

DISTRESSED
DAMSELFLY NYMPH

► **Adult Damselfly**
The common blue damsel (Enallagma spp.) displays its adult finery. Trout feed only occasionally on the winged adult form and ovipositing females.

AQUATICS *and* TERRESTRIALS

Hosts of aquatic creatures, such as snails, shrimp, and sculpins, are the basis of the trout's everyday diet, and all are essential for its survival. Carrying a selection of artificials of these creatures will give a solid foundation to your fly box and should be tried either when you are unsure which pattern you ought to fish next, or in early season before insects begin hatching in significant quantities.

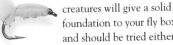

PEACH DOLL

Terrestrials, or land-based insects, also form part of the staple diet of trout. The scarcity of aquatic insects on many acidic waters means that these wind-blown tidbits are eagerly awaited by the trout, especially where the trees, bushes, and tall grasses from which the hapless terrestrials fall are close to the water.

On stillwaters during the autumn and winter there can be an explosion of activity, and large trout can become preoccupied by small fish.

▲ Water Flea
Daphnia are best imitated by largish flies that can represent a swarm, with bright orange or green in the dressing. Florescent peach is particularly enticing.

► Freshwater Shrimp
The ubiquitous freshwater shrimp is an ideal food form to imitate. Its colors vary from fawn and pink to greenish gray and orange-olive.

▲ Beetles
Beetles, such as this
coch-y-bondhu
(Phylloperta
horticola), live on
vegetation near the bank
and inadvertently fall or
are blown onto the
surface. An artificial with
peacock-herl body will
generally suffice,
although specific
imitations, such as the
coch-y-bondhu, exist.

▲ Bullhead
Relying on their stonelike coloration for camouflage,
the bullhead and the sculpin are chief among the
bottom-dwelling fish favored by trout. Big trout often
hunt for them at night. They are well imitated by the
Muddler Minnow.

▲ Ants
The winged version gives rise to
quite astonishing feeding during the
ant's mating period (mid- to late
summer). To omit ant patterns
from your fly box can result in
missed trout-catching
opportunities.

▲ Grasshoppers
The cricket and the grasshopper are
primarily of interest to the river fly fisher
and can frequently be found hopping
from bankside grasses onto the water.
Trout accept grasshoppers up to 2 in
(4 cm) in size.

ANT-FLY

BANKSIDE
EQUIPMENT
and SKILLS

SELECTING THE CORRECT rod, reel, line, and leader, tying the
right knot, and knowing how to employ subtle permutations
of your outfit to suit a variety of situations is crucial to
success. Equally, how to hook, play, land, and either kill or
release your quarry unharmed to the water are vital
elements of the sport. Understanding these aspects, along
with some basic safety pointers when wading in deep and
fast water, will enhance your enjoyment.

The Ultimate Fly Reel
*A small but substantial reel, this ATH Traum F1
incorporates sophisticated engineering.*

RIVER TACKLE

PRESENTATION, ACCURACY, and delicacy with occasional distance are prerequisites of the stream fisher. Choose your rod with the quarry, fly, and river size in mind, as well as the need for it to cope with obstacles such as overhanging bushes and trees or complicated currents. There are "cross overs," with some rods capable of covering large and small streams, even stillwaters. The perceived all-around river rod is 9 ft (3 m)/No. 4–5.

▲ **Small Rivers**
Light-line short rods are preferable when fishing with short casts into tight spots using fragile tippets and small flies. This example is a 7 ft (2 m)/ No. 3; perfect for brooks and overgrown streams.

▲ **Medium Rivers**
This 9 ft (3 m)/No. 4 outfit is an excellent example of an all-around dry fly and light nymph outfit capable of fishing size 22 flies on 6–7x tippets, while retaining the ability to handle trout in the 20 in (50 cm) class.

▲ **LargeRivers**
This 9 ft (3 m)/No. 7 rod is best suited to large wind-resistant flies and heavy nymphs. Excellent on small stillwaters when hunting larger specimens, and an ideal steelhead rod.

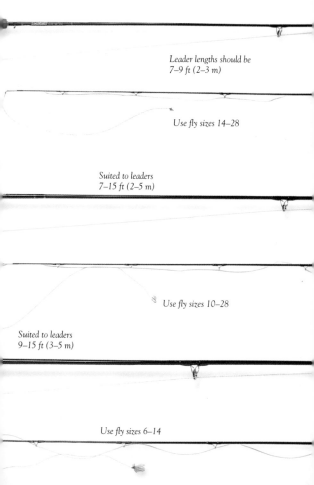

*Leader lengths should be
7–9 ft (2–3 m)*

Use fly sizes 14–28

*Suited to leaders
7–15 ft (2–5 m)*

Use fly sizes 10–28

*Suited to leaders
9–15 ft (3–5 m)*

Use fly sizes 6–14

LAKE, LOCH, *and* SALMON

I N FLY-FISHING, two areas benefit from the use of the longer rod – migratory fish and stillwater. A longer rod gives better control of terminal tackle and casting-related problems. It also effects roll-casts easier and will hold a fly longer in a taking lie on a salmon, sea trout, or steelhead river. It will also project higher back casts when boat fishing, fishing from a dam wall, and from the confines of a float tube.

▲ **Lake Fishing**
This 9 ft (3 m)/No. 6–7 rod is idea[l]
for stillwater bank fishing with
nymphs and small lures, and for bo[at]
fishing with dries and nymphs.

▶ **Loch Fishing**
Boat fishing calls for nearly continuous roll-
casting and dibbling of three or four flies on the
water. This 12 ft (4 m)/No. 6–7 rod makes the job
easier. It can also be used with a sunk line and
standard casting styles and is ideal as a light
summer salmon, sea trout, and grilse rod.

▲ **Salmon Fishing**
Being able to spey cast, fish
a sunk line, and swing a
weighted tube fly through lies
while keeping your line and fly
under control – this is essential to
salmon fishing. All can benefit from using a
longer rod, such as this 15 ft (5 m)/No. 10–11.

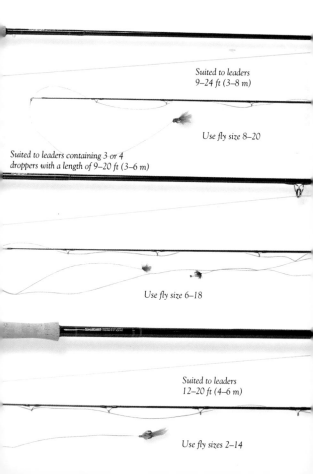

Suited to leaders
9–24 ft (3–8 m)

Use fly size 8–20

Suited to leaders containing 3 or 4
droppers with a length of 9–20 ft (3–6 m)

Use fly size 6–18

Suited to leaders
12–20 ft (4–6 m)

Use fly sizes 2–14

LINES *and* LEADERS

SELECTING THE RIGHT line is nearly as important as your choice of rod and probably more so than the reel. Balancing your outfit with the correct line weight to match the AFTM number written on the side of the rod is essential to placing the fly accurately at various distances and presenting the fly correctly. The leader should also be balanced and tapered to suit the type of water.

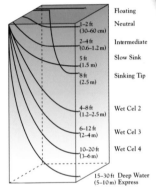

Floating

Neutral
1–2 ft
(30–60 cm)

Intermediate
2–4 ft
(0.6–1.2 m)

Slow Sink
5 ft
(1.5 m)

Sinking Tip
8 ft
(2.5 m)

Wet Cel 2
4–8 ft
(1.2–2.5 m)

Wet Cel 3
6–12 ft
(2–4 m)

Wet Cel 4
10–20 ft
(3–6 m)

Deep Water
15–30 ft
(5–10 m) Express

▶ **Covering Depths**
If you carry a wide range of line densities, you will be able to cover each layer from the surface to the bottom of rivers and stillwaters.

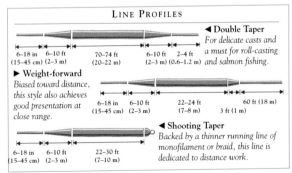

LINE PROFILES

◀ **Double Taper**
For delicate casts and a must for roll-casting and salmon fishing.

6–18 in (15–45 cm) 6–10 ft (2–3 m) 70–74 ft (20–22 m) 6–10 ft (2–3 m) 2–4 ft (0.6–1.2 m)

▶ **Weight-forward**
Biased toward distance, this style also achieves good presentation at close range.

6–18 in (15–45 cm) 6–10 ft (2–3 m) 22–24 ft (7–8 m) 3 ft (1 m) 60 ft (18 m)

◀ **Shooting Taper**
Backed by a thinner running line of monofilament or braid, this line is dedicated to distance work.

6–18 in (15–45 cm) 6–10 ft (2–3 m) 22–30 ft (7–10 m)

◀ Line Color
Floating lines come in every color from bright fluorescents to somber tans and grays. Bright lines are more visible and make bite detection easier, especially when nymph fishing. In clear water dry-fly situations use a drab color. Sinking lines should echo the muted hues of the subsurface world.

LEADERS AND TIPPETS

Your leader is the vital link between fly-line and fly. Selecting the right length, taper, and breaking strain of your leader determines the choice of fly size and delivery. Stillwater leaders are generally longer than those for rivers and offer the angler the option of fishing the fly at depth with a floating line. Remember, to fish a depth of 10 ft (3 m) you will need a leader of about 20 ft (6 m) to offset the angle of retrieve.

FLY-SIZE LONG SHANK	LEADER RATING (x)	BREAKING STRAIN (lb/kg)	DIAMETER (in/mm)
2–4	0x	14/6.36	.011/.282
4–6	1x	9/4.08	.010/.245
6–8	2x	7/3.17	.009/.220
8–10	3x	6/2.72	.008/.196
8–14	4x	5/2.26	.007/.171
12–18	5x	4/1.18	.006/.147
12–20	6x	3/1.36	.005/.122
18–28	7x	2/0.90	.004/.098
18–28	8x	1/0.45	.003/.073

SIMPLE LEADER

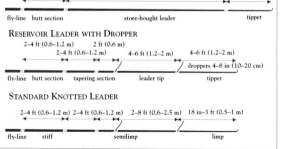

2–4 ft (0.6–1.2 m)   7–15 ft (2–5 m)   18 in–3 ft (0.5–1 m)

fly-line butt section   store-bought leader   tippet

RESERVOIR LEADER WITH DROPPER

2–4 ft (0.6–1.2 m)   2 ft (0.6 m)
   2–4 ft (0.6–1.2 m)   4–6 ft (1.2–2 m)   4–6 ft (1.2–2 m)

droppers 4–8 in (10–20 cm)

fly-line butt section   tapering section   leader tip   tippet

STANDARD KNOTTED LEADER

2–4 ft (0.6–1.2 m)   2–4 ft (0.6–1.2 m)   2–8 ft (0.6–2.5 m)   18 in–3 ft (0.5–1 m)

fly-line   stiff   semilimp   limp

KNOTS

T HE ABILITY to tie secure knots is fundamental in fishing. Although you need only a few to get by, you should get to know them intimately so that they can be tied quickly and correctly, even in half light.

Nylon is to some extent self-cutting and creates friction when pulled against itself. Get into the habit of moistening a knot with saliva, water, or a commercially available lubricant before tightening the knot.

Watch out for wind knots due to casting errors, which can reduce the nylon's breaking strain by 50 percent. Either retie a new tippet section or pick out the knot with a pin or hook point.

Here are the basic bankside knots. The Two Circle Turle will make your fly track absolutely straight through the water. Use the Double Grinner when joining nylon of different diameters.

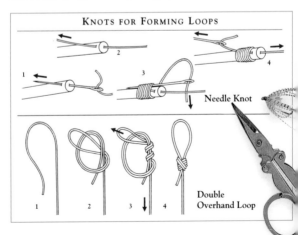

KNOTS FOR FORMING LOOPS

1 2 3 4

Needle Knot

Double
Overhand Loop

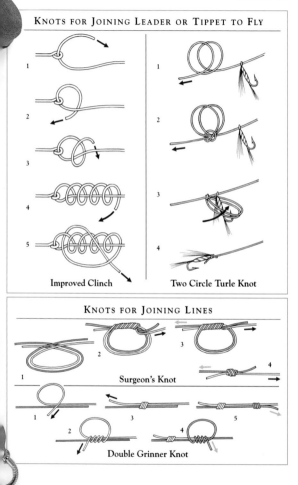

KNOTS FOR JOINING LEADER OR TIPPET TO FLY

1

2

3

4

5

Improved Clinch

1

2

3

4

Two Circle Turle Knot

KNOTS FOR JOINING LINES

1

2

3

4

Surgeon's Knot

1

2

3

4

5

Double Grinner Knot

CASTING TIPS

THE ABILITY TO place your fly exactly where you want it is the essence of successful fly-fishing. A good grounding is essential and professional lessons from a qualified instructor are the route to that goal. Always remember that fish tend to live in inaccessible places, so the ability to deliver your fly at long range, under bushes, or around obstacles with delicacy and accuracy will increase your chances immeasurably. The prerequisite is practice. Just as a golfer is constantly practicing swings, chips, and putts, so a cast improves with familiarity.

◄ **Bankside Cast**
Whether you are fishing still or moving water, aiming for a high delivery will improve your delicacy and distance – the cast will have greater opportunity to unfurl. Notice too how the elbow is kept in to the side, allowing the rod to become part of the fisher, rather than an afterthought.

◄ **Parachute Cast**
The parachute cast is made by aiming very high of the target, then suddenly lowering the rod, causing the fly and leader to flutter delicately water-ward. By aiming higher or lower you can alter the fly's descent. This cast is very useful when fishing downstream dry fly and in complicated currents, where the leader needs slack if drag is not to set in immediately.

THE SINGLE SPEY CAST
Once mastered, you will seldom need another cast when salmon fishing, or where high banks and overhang are encountered during trout fishing.

1 It really is best to practice this cast on moving water since the lines "pull" and "drag" against the current. Start with the line below you and begin by raising your rod tip, lifting some of the line from the surface. Then move it in a fairly quick movement to the upstream side of you. Notice the hand position during the movement of the line from downstream.

2 Change the balance from the right to the left – it is a good idea to have the foot facing in the direction of the cast and the right hand up the rod. As the angler in this sequence is on the true right bank he must alter the grip so that the left hand is uppermost.

3 By punching the shoulders, drive the rod tip fast and high, allowing the line to travel across the river. Do not let the rod butt stray too far from your body – it should be positioned at about heart level. Practice this cast with a floating line and remember – timing throughout is critical.

PLAYING *and* LANDING

H AVING HOOKED YOUR quarry, you now have to ensure that it does not get away. Playing the fish should be done quickly, positively, and with confidence. In the case of large trout and salmon, overgrown bankside areas and fast currents, play your fish "on the reel," using the rim and drag settings to control and tire the fish.

◄**Playing a Fish**
By keeping the rod near to the vertical, much of the shock of a fish's sudden movements will be absorbed by the rod tip, protecting the hook hold and tippet. Apply side strain to turn a fast-running fish.

LANDING YOUR CATCH

Netting is the easiest method of landing a fish. Always ensure that the net is large enough; use knotless mesh whenever you intend to return your quarry to the water.

1 *Start by submerging the net in the water. Always lead the fish to the net and try to get on the downstream side of your catch. Find a hazard-free landing area if at all possible.*

2 Once the quarry is over the center of the net, lift it so that the fish is swallowed up in the mesh folds. A round net with a metal rim will help retrieve fish from a variety of angles and obstructions, such as weed beds.

3 Never lift the net by the handle when landing a large fish; the head lock could collapse. Instead, grasp the net at the junction of the head and handle, lift and twist it, then bring the fish onto the bank.

▲ Killing
Always respect your quarry. Once it is safely on the bank, hit it on the head above the eyes once or twice with a small club.

RELEASING *your* CATCH

ONE OF THE HIGHLIGHTS of angling is to release your quarry back into the wild to live and perhaps fight another day. Always release your catch with the utmost care. Dry hands, harsh netting, prolonged handling, and stones on the bank will damage the delicate membrane covering the scales, opening the way for infection and disease. Trauma will also affect a fish that has been played or kept out of the water too long. Your prerogative is to respect your quarry, your care being essential to the creature's well-being.

GRAY GOOSE

RELEASING HUMANELY

As soon as a fish is taken from the water, stress sets in. If you want a photographic record of your prize, have the camera already set up.

1 *Having swiftly brought your fish in, gently cradle and support it. Never squeeze the fish with your hands. If it struggles, turn it gently upside down and it will stop fighting, allowing you to extract the hook easily.*

REMOVING THE HOOK

Fingers, forceps, and even rod tips can be used to remove a hook. Whatever method you intend to employ, make certain it causes no damage or stress and is speedy.

Rod Tip Removal
This humane technique can be used only with barbless hooks. Simply push your rod tip downward against the hook (right). Jag forward and the hook will come out. Do this while the fish is still in the water.

Barbless or microbarb hooks will help enormously. A barbed hook can quickly be rendered barbless by squeezing down the barb with smooth-jawed pliers or forceps.

2 Having disengaged the hook, it is time to release the fish. At the riverside, always ensure that its head is facing the current. Cradle your catch in the water until it has sufficient strength to "kick" out of your hands, even if it takes 20 or more minutes. Never rush this process – the fish's life depends on it. Also, never let the fish go belly up after release, because it will die.

TIPS for SAFETY

How precious is your life? Care when wading should take priority over everything, and a few golden rules must always be observed. Always let someone know where you are. If the water looks difficult, fish in pairs. Wear felt-soled waders on slippery surfaces. Use a wading staff in strong currents, and carry a whistle to alert people. If you have a flotation vest – and you should – always wear it.

PROCEED WITH CAUTION

Any river or stillwater is a potential hazard. With a little common sense, however, even fast currents can be safely negotiated. Stay alert for changes in the current, or at the bottom, which suggest that the area is altering. If in doubt use a wading staff for support. Remember, as well as the obvious danger, any fall will also frighten off your quarry.

▲ **Danger Point**
Putting all your balance on one foot, as shown here, is exactly what you should not do. Any slight depression or large obstacle on the river bed could upend you. Always balance yourself on both feet and move one foot in front of the other to search out obstacles with the toe of your boot.

▲ **Turning in the Current**
Turning in any current is ill-advised, as is facing downstream in all but the gentlest of currents – an unseen object could knock you over. This angler has balanced himself to cause least resistance to the flow, even though facing downstream.

▶ The Contented Angler
The current is easy, the depth is constant, the river bed relatively trouble-free. But even here care must be taken – a mistimed step could lead to a cold bath or worse. Nevertheless, this fly fisher is facing the current, and his neoprene waders not only afford a degree of buoyancy but also warmth and protection.

STAYING AFLOAT

The impact of a fall will drive you below the surface. Don't panic. If you are not wearing a buoyancy device, get your head to the surface, stretch your arms out to form a "crucifix" position, and ride the current downstream. Stay calm and gently maneuver yourself to the bank with small, steering hand movements. Once on dry land, roll onto your back and raise both legs to empty your waders. Remember, hypothermia can set in even in warm weather. Have a warm drink and change into dry clothing as soon as possible.

WATER
and TACTICS

AS IMPORTANT AS UNDERSTANDING the quarry is
knowing how to deceive the trout with a combination of
watercraft, casting skill, tactics, and selection of the right fly
pattern for the job. All are essential for a rewarding
outcome. The following pages explain how to choose the
ideal tackle and flies and apply the correct tactics for the
various game-fishing disciplines. Although not exhaustive,
there is sufficient advice and guidance here to help
you fish successfully for game fish in most kinds
of water around the world.

To Rise a Trout
*Using the weed bed to break up and camouflage his
approach, the fly fisher slides a cast between the channels,
relying on pinpoint casting accuracy to fool the trout.*

LOCATING FISH *in* SPRING CREEKS

THERE IS A CONSISTENCY about spring creeks. The current tends to be placid and even, weeds grow abundantly, and the depth does not reach the same highs and lows as freestone rivers. Nevertheless, fish find the environment very much to their liking due to the rivers' alkaline-suffused richness.

Pay particular attention to the verdant margins. Channels between the weed beds are classic lies because the constant stream of food, coupled with the ever-present comfort of cover, make the channels the perfect location. Be aware of hatch pools (where some of the largest fish congregate), undercut banks, and bridges. Because of the usual ultraclear water conditions, it is easy to imagine that locating fish will be straightforward. Remember, if you can see them, they can see you, so dress somberly and tread with caution.

WATER CLARITY

Remember that any fish you spot in the extremely clear spring creek water can also see you, and from a considerable distance. Therefore, it is sometimes better to cast from a kneeling position, particularly when there is no bankside cover.

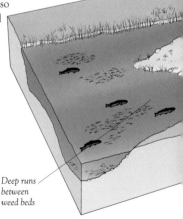

Deep runs between weed beds

▶ Weed Channels

Channels between the weeds are a favorite holding spot. Trout sheltering in these places have a tendency to be more nervous because of their exposed position. Careful casting, wading, and presentation are therefore essential.

Pool

Bridge

Undercut bank

Feeder stream

Exposed shallows

▲ Spring Creek Lies

Certain features in a spring creek, such as bridges or undercut banks, are particularly attractive to trout, but most areas are worth trying. In pools, trout tend to face downstream because of the current reversal that occurs in the eddies.

TIPS *for* SPRING CREEKS

MOST FLY FISHERS of spring-fed rivers agree that how anglers present themselves is almost as important as the way they fish the fly. To stand bolt upright wearing white or brightly colored clothing and stride boldly along the bank is inviting disaster. Fishing spring creeks is somewhat like jungle warfare, where a crack from a broken twig sounds the alarm and can alert the enemy to your presence. To be successful you must try to harmonize with the surroundings. Clothing should therefore echo rather than fight with the colors around you. Against a backdrop of grass and blue sky, wear lighter colors; with trees or bushes in the background, clothing should likewise be darker.

KEY TO SUCCESS

Apart from approach, the next vital element is delicate and accurate casting. It is often said that you can get away with fairly inaccurate flies just as long as your presentation is on target; an inch either way can be the difference between success and failure.

A

Slack-line parachute cast – current will straighten out line

Tight, downstream and across cast – a shorter drift before fly starts to drag

◀ **Wading Cautiously**
Even when wading in a stream, exercise caution. Utilize the surroundings to break up your silhouette. Weed beds or rafts will obscure you from the fish's subsurface vision. Don't be afraid to cast across a weed mat – this can be the ultimate deceitful presentation. Above all, avoid heavy footfalls.

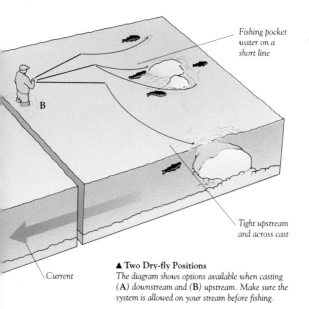

Fishing pocket water on a short line

Tight upstream and across cast

Current

▲ **Two Dry-fly Positions**
*The diagram shows options available when casting (**A**) downstream and (**B**) upstream. Make sure the system is allowed on your stream before fishing.*

SPRING CREEK FLY HATCHES

The chart details the seasonal fly hatches and suggests artificial flies that can be used at the appropriate times.

Always remember to abide by the local fishing season

	Mayflies 1/16–1 1/4 in (2–30 mm)	Caddis 1/4–1 1/4 in (5–30 mm)
JANUARY		
FEBRUARY		
MARCH	░	
APRIL	▒	░
MAY	▓	▒
JUNE	▓	▓
JULY	▒	▓
AUGUST	▓	▓
SEPTEMBER	▓	▒
OCTOBER	░	░
NOVEMBER		
DECEMBER		
SUGGESTED ARTIFICIALS: (*Some flies are effective for multiple naturals.*)	Sawyer's Pheasant Tail GE Nymph Baetid Nymph Mayfly Nymph Duck's Dun Transition Dun No Hackle Dun Rust Spinner	Stick Fly Hare's Ear (Flashback) Rhyacophila Larva Grannom Pupa Silver Invicta Balloon Caddis Micro Caddis Tent Wing Caddis Realistic Caddis

Light activity – sporadic feeding
Increased activity – regular feeding
Heavy activity – heavy feeding
Intense activity – intense preoccupied feeding

Terrestrials 1/4–1 1/2 in (5–40 mm)	**Crustaceans** 1/4–3/4 in (5–15 mm)	**Midges** 1/4–3/4 in (5–15 mm)
McMurray Ant Ethafoam Beetle Halford Black Gnat Dave's Hopper Coch-y-bondhu	Red Spot Shrimp Killer Bug Hare's Ear (Flashback) Troth Pheasant Tail	San Juan Worm Bead Head Brassie Serendipity Tube Buzzer Lurex Spider Goddard's Suspender Pupa Halford Black Gnat

SPRING CREEK NYMPHS

T HE TERM "NYMPH," in this instance, is very ambiguous. It could mean either the Skues'esque emergers that caused controversy at the turn of the century, or the deeply sunk versions codified by Sawyer during the 1940s and 1950s, which continued a French tradition started in 1873. However you interpret the term, this range of flies is deadly when fished to an observed quarry in the upstream, dead-drift manner. In almost all cases, nymph fishing is permitted. The standard (Std) or long shank (Ls) hook sizes are given throughout.

Ls 14–18

Baetid Nymph
This design by Ollie Edwards is an ultra-realistic pattern that imitates various upwing nymphs. Fish upstream and dead-drift into the feeding zone.

Std 14–20

Tom's Bead Head
This Pheasant Tail variation by the legendary Tom Travis can be very effective when fished upstream, dead-drifted through pocket water, and holding lies.

Std 12–18

Sawyer's Pheasant Tail
This highly effective pattern could catch trout almost irrespective of water type. It uses the fibers from the tail of a cock pheasant and a length of dark copper wire.

Std 10–20

Goddard's Suspender Pupa
Midge pupae are very important for spring creek fishing, and this pattern is indispensable when trout are feeding on the natural.

Std 12–18

GE Nymph
Broadly representational of a wide spectrum of upwinged nymphs, this pattern can be fished with confidence upstream and dead-drifted.

Std 10–16

Red Spot Shrimp
A shrimp pattern with fluorescent red wool spots. Broadly appealing, though only where freshwater crustaceans occur.

Std 12–24

Brassie

One of the best all-around nymph patterns you could carry. Great on stillwater as well as rivers, fish it upstream but allow it to sway slightly.

Std 12–24

Serendipity

One of America's favorite surface pupa patterns for midge or caddis. The deer hair collar keeps it in the film. Fish it dead-drift.

Std 10–14

Killer Bug

A rather nondescript, maggot-shaped fly made of darning wool, but nonetheless successful. Trout may mistake it for shrimp or caddis.

Std 12–18

Floating Nymph (Jardine)

This style is quite familiar, but the addition of a parachute hackle has increased its allure. Fish up- or downstream, dead-drift, without drag.

Std 10–16

Hare's Ear (Flashback)

This pattern covers all seasons. You could confidently fish this indispensable pattern in any water, in most styles, and expect to catch fish.

Std 12–16

Grannom Pupa

The grannom is the first caddis to hatch. Although designed for the beginning of the season, this pattern works well all year round for olive-bodied caddis.

Std 12–16

Gray Goose

Lady Amherst pheasant has been used instead of herl-fiber tail. Best fished upstream, dead-drift, in the classic Nether-Avon style.

Ls 8–12

Mayfly Nymph

This pattern is so effective when the naturals are not present that many fishers wonder just what trout take it for. Dick Walker created this long-shank nymph, which appears to be as good on rivers as on stillwater. It is truly ubiquitous.

SPRING CREEK DRY FLIES

Most people's idea of dry-fly fishing is that of a crystal stream, snaking its way through a lush, green, sleepy valley, with trout casually dimpling the surface as they lift in the current. Even though most of the trout's food will be sub-surface, the dense hatches tend to ensure that fish in alkaline waters spend a good deal of their time looking surfaceward. The small collection shown here will, if carried in various sizes, deceive trout and grayling the world over.

Std 16–20

Halford Black Gnat
Frederick Halford was a dry-fly purist and a superb flytier. This Halford pattern represents Bibio johannis, a midge that occurs frequently on spring creeks.

Std 14–24

Rust Spinner
This Bonnie and René Harrop pattern uses hackle fibers at the thorax area. It represents the pale morning dun and blue-winged olive. Use when fish feed on spinners.

Std 18–24

AK Parachute
Conceived by A.K. Best, this pattern is most effective presented on fine 7x tippets to ultrashy fish feeding on Baetis duns. Can also be used purely as a searching pattern when you are uncertain.

Std 16–22

No Hackle Dun
When fish are feeding in the surface film or on hatching or newly hatched duns, this is the fly to use. It is an excellent low-riding and flush pattern.

Std 16–24

Transition Dun
This René Harrop pattern is a particularly effective imitator of a mayfly between the nymph and adult stages. Fish on fine tippets to sipping risers.

Std 16–20

Chalk Dun
Though difficult to tie, this freshly emerged olive dressing can be deadly on ultraselective trout. Ideal in flat water situations. Use fine tippets and long leaders.

Std 16–18

McMurray Ant

Trout just love terrestrials, often picking them out amid a heavy hatch of duns. This pattern is the ultimate ant imitator.

Std 10–20

Tent Wing Caddis

One of the original close-copy designs that remain effective whenever trout are selectively feeding on caddis in calm areas. Best fished dead-drift.

Std 16–22

Glitter Spinner

Primarily for evening fishing, this bright orange imitation of the mayfly's last stage can deceive fish that have ignored standard patterns.

Std 16–22

Micro Caddis

Created on the banks of Montana rivers, this sleek, delicate-bodied caddis pattern is best fished dead-drift to rising trout, on light tippets, toward dusk.

Std 16–18

Beacon Beige

The Americans have the Gulper Adams, the British this essential fly. More sparse than its American cousin, it remains one of the best adult-olive imitations.

Std 12–20

Gulper Adams

Very often trout expect flies to be stuck in the surface film. This pattern does just that while at the same time the wing offers a very good visual aid. Low-riding.

Std 14–22

Sparkle Dun

This pattern was first shown to me by John Goddard. I became curious after his fifth grayling weighing over 2 lb (1 kg). It is a low-riding and flush pattern.

Std 12–24

Duck's Dun

This is my all-purpose fly when duns hatch. By varying the body color all species can be covered with one type of dressing. Best for trout feeding at the surface.

Std 10–16

Realistic Caddis

Every now and again you need a pattern close to the original but sufficiently "buggy" to attract fish to the surface. Use this one in the evening around trees and under cut banks.

FREESTONE TACTICS

BECAUSE OF THE RIVER'S turbulent nature, it is easy to fall into the trap of thinking that caution or tactics are not necessary. Often, you will not see your quarry clearly; the fish, nevertheless, will rise at appropriate times, calling on you to present a dry fly drag-free to stand any chance at all. When you fish with nymphs or wet flies, you must adopt a rational, searching approach through likely areas such as riffles, runs, pools, or pockets. Intimate knowledge of your river is essential, so give yourself time to assess each section before fishing.

Casting Upstream
On the variety of currents offered by freestone rivers, "upstream" is still the best method of presenting dry, wet, and nymph in most instances. Here, the angler is fishing the pocket of water provided by a boulder. In front, to the side, and behind are all prime targets.

CURRENT

dipping point

Watch indicator for any evidence of a take

indicator

Cast is made upstream of a visible fish or its assumed position

To keep in touch with nymph, retrieve line at same speed as current

UPSTREAM

◄ A Freestone Pool
Not all freestone river
areas are raging torrents.
Pools can be among the
most productive places in
the river system. The
tranquil sides are favored
by trout during dawn and
dusk. Using a small dry
fly, especially a spinner
pattern, can be deadly.
Do not overlook using
a streamer.

KEY TO SUCCESS

For all methods of presentation,
line control is essential when
fishing in slack or fast areas.
By altering your rod's angle, or
retrieving line at the same speed
as the current, you will keep in
contact with your pattern.
Remember, trout and grayling
tend to hit a fly much faster on
freestone rivers. Be prepared to
strike instantaneously.

A high rod position
means less line/water
drag and a faster strike

Keep as much line as
possible off surface

FREESTONE TACTICS (Continued)

FISHING DOWNSTREAM

There are times when fishing upstream may not be possible. Long drifting a dry fly downstream, or a down-and-across wet-style, can also be effective. When using a dry fly downstream, look for a riffle or run 2–4 ft (60 cm–1.2 m) deep. A choppy riffle 1 ft (30 cm) deep would be best for a wet fly.

INDUCING A TAKE

Trout find flies that rise in front of their noses hard to resist. To induce a take in this way, you must be able to see the fish and make the fly rise at the right time. Let a weighted fly sink to the trout's holding depth, then lift the fly by raising the rod as it nears the fish.

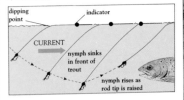

dipping point   indicator

CURRENT

nymph sinks in front of trout

nymph rises as rod tip is raised

Wading on a freestone river can be vital to place you in the best position. The two anglers illustrated below show two distinctly different strategies. On the left, a dry fly or nymph is being fished downstream with a periodic halting of its progress. This causes the fly to stutter or suddenly rise up in the manner of a real fly about to hatch. On the right, the angler is casting upstream and allowing the current to pull a nymph, streamer, or team of wet flies in a sweeping arc. Takes on this style are fleeting, so be ready.

Each time line is checked, nymph swings invitingly upward or causes a dry fly to skitter

drift

▶ **The Perfect Freestone Stretch**
Where the water is only knee-high it can be ideal for both dry fly and nymph fishing. With a fairly gentle riffle, it provides superb conditions for emerging insects and feeding game fish alike. When you come across a stretch of water like this, remember not to rush things.

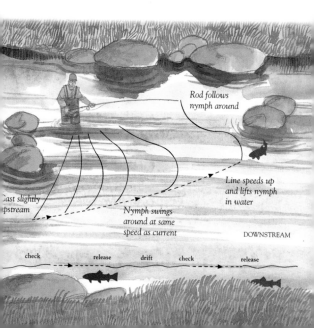

Rod follows nymph around

Line speeds up and lifts nymph in water

Cast slightly upstream

Nymph swings around at same speed as current

DOWNSTREAM

check   release   drift   check   release

FREESTONE FLY HATCHES

The chart details the seasonal fly hatches and suggests artificial flies that can be used at the appropriate times.

Always remember to abide by the local fishing season

	Mayflies 1/16–1 1/4 in (2–30 mm)	Caddis 1/4–1 1/4 in (5–30 mm)	Stoneflies 3/4–3 in (15–80 mm)
JANUARY			
FEBRUARY			
MARCH	░		░
APRIL	▒	░	▒
MAY	▓	▒	▒
JUNE	▓	▓	░
JULY	▓	▓	░
AUGUST	▒	▓	▒
SEPTEMBER	▓	▒	
OCTOBER	░		
NOVEMBER			
DECEMBER			
SUGGESTED ARTIFICIALS: (Some flies are effective for multiple naturals.)	GE Nymph Baetid Nymph Mayfly Nymph Duck's Dun Transition Dun No Hackle Dun Rust Spinner March Brown	Stick Fly Brassie Gold Head Pupa Rhyacophila Larva Moser Caddis Pupa Deep Olive Pupa Klinkhammer Special Realistic Caddis	Woolly Bugger Girdle Bug Woven Stonefly Bead Head Prince Troth Pheasant Tail Partridge & Orange Stimulator Yellow Humpy

Light activity – sporadic feeding
Increased activity – regular feeding
Heavy activity – heavy feeding
Intense activity – intense preoccupied feeding

Terrestrials 1/4–1 1/2 in (5–40 mm)	Crustaceans 1/4–3/4 in (5–15 mm)	Midges 1/4–3/4 in (5–15 mm)	Fish 3/4–3 in (15–80 mm)
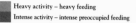			
Ethafoam Beetle	Red Spot Shrimp	San Juan Worm	Flat Head Sculpin
Coch-y-bondhu	Killer Bug	Bead Head Brassie	Woolly Bugger
Renegade	Hare's Ear	Serendipity	Bead Head Prince
McMurray Ant	(Flashback)	Tube Buzzer	Minky
Dave's Hopper	Troth Pheasant Tail	Lurex Spider	Muddler Minnow
		Goddard's Suspender Pupa	
		Halford Black Gnat	

FREESTONE SUNK

W█HILE ABOVE THE SURFACE may be white-water madness and turmoil, things can be entirely different below. Game fish in freestone rivers tend to look at life rather differently – a case of "grab while you can" as opposed to "select and inspect, eat or reject." Life on these rivers generally moves fast, making the calmer pockets and little depressions important feeding grounds. The importance of aquatic creatures should not be overlooked – fish, worms, and all kinds of insects come under the scrutiny of a hungry trout.

Std 10–14

Moser Caddis Pupa
A simple, easy-to-tie pupa pattern that is, nevertheless, deadly. Fish in all kinds of flows, just beneath the surface, when the naturals are on the wing.

Std 10–14

Rhyacophila Larva
Ollie Edwards' close copy of a favorite trout and grayling subsurface snack. Fish this singularly, near the bottom with weighted leaders or by adding lead.

Std 10–16

Deep Olive Pupa
Gary LaFontaine's fly patterns indicate his extensive knowledge of caddis. Antron, a material to which air bubbles cling, is used to imitate the natural fly.

Std 12–18

Partridge & Orange
A classic wet fly of fast rocky river origin. When fished early season, across and down, it is ideal for rough-stream trout and grayling.

Std 10–12

March Brown
Here I have darkened Al Troth's original body color and used hare's fur tinged with red. Fish in areas of large boulders and medium flow, near to the bottom.

Std 10–18

Troth Pheasant Tail
Any fly from Al Troth is worth including in a fly box. The use of peacock herl for the thorax gives the fly a slightly midge-like air and a bit of sparkle.

Std 10–16

Gold Head Pupa

The Gold Head can be gold-plated or, if a more realistic, clear-water type is required, brass is a better choice. Fish this pattern dead-drift on a floating line and long leader.

Ls 8–14

Bead Head Prince

The addition of a gold head has enhanced this already deadly all-purpose nymph. Fish dead-drift, or twitched near to the bottom of both fast-running or slack areas.

Std 12–16

San Juan Worm

This fly is deadly for both aquatic worms and Chironomid larva, fished dead-drift with sufficient ballast to place the pattern near the bottom of the river.

Ls 2–12

Girdle Bug

This impressionistic pattern of a large stonefly nymph is good in fast, boisterous water, which moves the rubber legs. Fish heavily leaded, around boulders and close to the bottom. A favorite on Rocky Mountain rivers.

Ls 4–10

Woven Stonefly

This pattern is a fairly close copy of the larger stoneflies that live in fast riffles and glides. Fish dead-drift near to the bottom with either weighted leaders or by adding lead.

Ls 2–12

Woolly Bugger

One of the best modern creations. Designed by Russell Blessing, its role embraces that of bait-fish imitation, damsel nymph, dragonfly nymph, and other nymphs in small sizes. It is also a plain attractor of trout.

Ls 2–12

Flat Head Sculpin

Sculpin are feeding targets for trout. Very much a freestone fly, lake and reservoir fish may also respond to its use. The head is flattened to give a unique swimming movement. Fish on a sinking-tip line, down and across.

FREESTONE DRY

IMPORTANT AS the subsurface fly is on freestone rivers, fishing dry can be more effective, and certainly more fun. There are many flies that hatch onto the surface, but augmenting these are a good number of terrestrial forms. One of the biggest problems, however, is seeing your fly amid the confused currents. A parachute pattern, with a white or fluorescent wing, can enhance visual contact while allowing the trout optimum vision on the underside.

Std 12–16

Coch-y-bondhu
This classic Welsh beetle pattern is representative of insects very much in evidence throughout the summer on particularly rough streams and acidic lakes.

Std 14–18

Tup's Indispensable
This commercial pattern is named after the wool coming from a tup's (ram's) hindquarters. It is a superb, pale watery pattern originated by R.S. Austin.

Std 8–16

Elk Hair Caddis
The fluorescent yellow butt echoes the female caddis's egg cluster. It works extremely well when natural adult caddis are around, especially during late evening.

Std 10–14

Balloon Caddis
This pattern represents caddis emerging and hanging in the surface film. Fish dead-drift on a floating line and buoyant leader.

Std 10–18

Ethafoam Beetle
The foam back keeps this pattern afloat in the surface film, imitating the natural, while the dubbed body offers an illusion of life.

Std 10–16

Klinkhammer Special
One of the most popular rough-water dry flies for trout, and especially for grayling, this pattern imitates caddis and should be fished dead-drift.

Std 10–14

Renegade
*This fly is unusual in that
a hackle is placed at the
bend of the hook and,
conventionally, to the
fore. It is rated as one of
the top rainbow trout flies.*

Std 12–18

Parachute Hare's Ear
*Similar to Klinkhammer,
the white wing offers
maximum visibility in low
light or rough water while
giving a caddislike profile
from below.*

Std 10–18

Parachute Royal Wulff
*One of the finest fast-
water, maximum
visibility attractor
patterns available. Good
for all waters. Best fished
upstream, dead-drift.*

Std 10–14

H & L Variant
*This is a great favorite
with Western anglers as a
search pattern in fast
turbulent water. Often
fished with a small
nymph, trailed from
nylon and attached to the
head band.*

Std 10–16

Yellow Humpy
*Universally popular with
fly fishers in the US. In
England I have enjoyed
great success with it,
especially as a hatching
mayfly pattern. Always
carry in all sizes to cover
most freestone situations.*

Ls 6–12

Stimulator
*This Randall Kaufmann
fly covers stoneflies and
terrestrials such as
hoppers and caddis flies.
A good general fly, it also
covers many floating-fly
requirements.*

Std 4–12

Dave's Hopper
*One of America's most
innovative flytiers, Dave
Whitlock has achieved
good floating properties
through inspired use of
deer hair.*

Std 4–10

Moser's Adult Stone
*Roman Moser's use of natural and man-
made materials is first rate. His organza-
designed wing is fused with a dubbed body
of deer hair. A pattern for dead-drift
situations more than skittering fish.
Fish up- or downstream.*

LOCATING FISH *in* STILLWATER

FINDING THE QUARRY on a seemingly featureless and clue-free piece of water is more than half the battle. There will of course be times when trout give themselves away by rising, but this is seldom the norm. There can be no substitute for getting to know a stretch of water over a period of time. By seeing it under a variety of conditions and seasons, a sound picture will build up of fish-holding areas, which may vary from month to month. You will know the deeps, insect-rich weed beds, productive shallows, depressions, gullies, underwater plateaus, and so on.

There are, of course, vital clues even for the visiting fisher, and by walking the banks prior to fishing – even over a comparatively small area – an excellent "feel" for the water and subsurface terrain will allow areas to be tackled with reasonable confidence.

KEY TO SUCCESS

If you intend fishing a lake for the first time, ask a local for advice on the best spots, insect hatches, and the types of tackle usually employed on that water. Don't forget to take a pair of binoculars, as they will help spy out areas and scan the water for signs of rising trout.

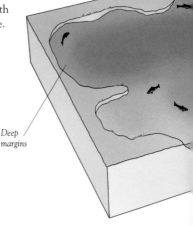

Deep margins

◀ Low Profile
*Even on stillwater caution is a good
idea, especially at times such as
dawn, evening, and those periods of
the season when trout hunt the
shoreline. A crouched angler is far
less visible and invariably more
successful. Of course this does not
apply when trout seek the cool depths
during heat waves and harsh light, or
the warmth of deep water during cold
snaps. But when fish are nymphing or
sipping dry flies – fish fine and gentle
and keep low.*

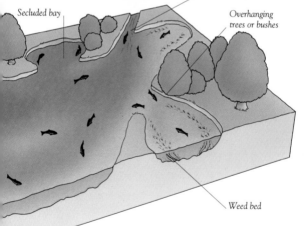

Inflow or outflow stream

Secluded bay

*Overhanging
trees or bushes*

Weed bed

▲ Typical Small Stillwater
*The areas indicated are always good starting points and
are generally fish-holding areas. By shunning the crowd,
you will locate quarry that will venture into undisturbed
shallow water if the conditions are conducive.*

BANK FISHING

FISHING THE SHORELINE of any stillwater demands tactics that may have to change from season to season, week to week, and even hour to hour. To meet this challenge,

Leaping Rise
Trout are often seen hurling themselves out of the water in pursuit of large insects, especially during high summer.

you will have to vary your approach. By varying lines and leader lengths a great many depths can be explored. Remember that for fishing the bottom roughly twice as much leader is required because of the retrieve angle.

There are times when you will need a pattern fished on a subsurface flat plane, such as to imitate damsel nymph activity. This will require an intermediate or sinking tip line. Similarly, in the early-season cold, when fish are slow to respond and lying deep, you may need a fast-sinking line and a buoyant fly that hugs the lake floor. In these conditions fish slowly. Versatility and an open mind are the keys to successful bank fishing.

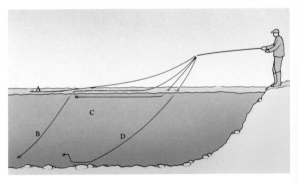

HOLDING SPOTS IN A RESERVOIR

The observant angler should be able to ascertain where fish are likely to congregate in a large expanse of water. Look for clues that suggest submerged features; these areas tend to attract fish due to the accumulation of food.

Dam wall

Sloping bank

Submerged trees

Submerged fences and hedges

Submerged roads and ditches

▶ **Favorite Haunts**
Shallow, weedy shelves by the bank soon warm up in the early season and contain a variety of insects to tempt fish. Deeper water beyond provides sanctuary and comfortable feeding conditions year-round.

◀ **Bank-Fishing Lines**
Floating line and suspended fly for surface film (A), floating line and long leader (B), slow or intermediate line for windy conditions and mid-water feeders (C), Wet Cel 4 line and buoyant fly on a short leader (D).

FLOAT-TUBING

ORIGINALLY DEVELOPED IN the US during the late 1880s, this flipper-propelled, specially designed, truck-sized inner tube is easily transportable and enables the angler to explore lakes more thoroughly. Several important rules must always be observed – only use a float tube if you are a proficient swimmer, wear a flotation device, always enter the water at the farthest point downwind, do not venture further than 100 yd (91 m) from the shoreline, if possible fish in pairs, do not go out in strong wind or rough conditions, and only fish in short bursts if you are new to tubing.

Raquet-style landing net

Float tube

Apron

Flippers

▲ **The Tube in Action**
The apron in front stops the retrieved line from falling into the tube and becoming entangled in the angler's legs; it also provides a shelf to rest your catch or equipment on when changing systems.

Wind direction

Paddle upwind and across

Cast downwind

Fly curves around

▶ **The Nymph Swing**
Paddling upwind and across allows the line to curve across the surface of the water. This approach can be particularly effective if midges, olives, damsels, or caddis are becoming active and you spy fish moving.

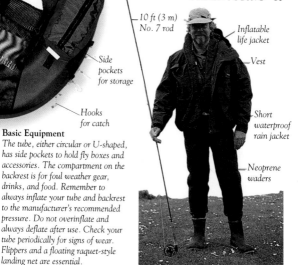

_10 ft (3 m)_
No. 7 rod

Inflatable
life jacket

Vest

Side
pockets
for storage

Hooks
for catch

Short
waterproof
rain jacket

Neoprene
waders

Basic Equipment
The tube, either circular or U-shaped, has side pockets to hold fly boxes and accessories. The compartment on the backrest is for foul weather gear, drinks, and food. Remember to always inflate your tube and backrest to the manufacturer's recommended pressure. Do not overinflate and always deflate after use. Check your tube periodically for signs of wear. Flippers and a floating raquet-style landing net are essential.

LINES FOR TUBE FISHING

When fishing from a float tube, always carry a a good range of line densities. This will enable all layers, from surface to bottom, to be covered effectively. The illustration shows how a shelving bank, dam wall, or gully can be searched at all depths by varying the line type. Sunk lines also enable you to fish patterns in a gradually descending curve, something that trout tend to find particularly enticing.

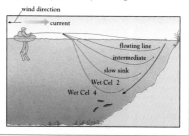

wind direction

current

floating line

intermediate

slow sink

Wet Cel 2

Wet Cel 4

BOAT TACTICS

THERE ARE MANY different styles of boat fishing, ranging from plain anchoring to perhaps the most pleasurable – loch-style. In the truest sense, fishing loch-style involves using an almost permanently retrieved team of three or four flies on a short line, with a 11 ft (3.36 m) rod, to the front of a broadside drifting boat. Now, longer line techniques are employed, using both floating and sunk lines. Traditional wet flies, nymphs, and lures are used, along with dry flies and emergers.

KEY TO SUCCESS

Dusk and dawn are the best times to fish loch-style. At such insect-rich times, drift through rising trout and cover with static dry flies or slowly fished nymphs. During the classic conditions of low cloud, a gentle rolling wave, and a warm airstream, the wet fly comes into its own.

Using a Drogue
A drogue is rather like an underwater parachute, attached to the rear of the boat by a 5–15 ft (1.5–4.5 m) length of rope. In adverse, windy conditions, the drogue slows down the boat's drift, allowing you to keep up with your flies.

LOCH-STYLE METHODS – FISHING THE DRIFT

With a floating line

Balancing the leader is very important. The heaviest fly should be placed on the point position to anchor the team. The bushiest fly, the one that will cause the most disturbance, should go on the top-dropper. At the middle position try a sparse wet fly or nymph. An important factor is always to retrieve faster, even if only fractionally faster, than the drifting speed of the boat.

With a sunk line

The sunk line allows you to explore a variety of depths in one cast,

using the strip-and-hang technique. Cast as far downwind as possible (**A**), allow the line to settle, giving a sharp tug to straighten if needed (**B**). Allow the line to descend (**C**), keeping in touch with the line by slowly retrieving the slack to the desired depth. Now lift the rod, stopping periodically at different levels (**D**). Takes very often occur throughout the movement upward, especially as you hold. When you see the end of your fly line (**E**), hold indefinitely, as very often this is when the trout takes. It is not unusual to hold the position for a minute or more.

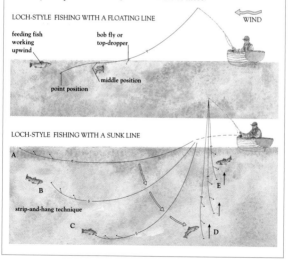

LOCH-STYLE FISHING WITH A FLOATING LINE

WIND

feeding fish working upwind

bob fly or top-dropper

point position

middle position

LOCH-STYLE FISHING WITH A SUNK LINE

A

B

strip-and-hang technique

C

D

E

STILLWATER FLY HATCHES

The chart details the seasonal fly hatches and suggests artificial flies that can be used at the appropriate times.

Always remember to abide by the local fishing season

	Midges ¼–¾ in (5–15 mm)	Caddis ¼–1¼ in (5–30 mm)	Mayflies ¹⁄₁₆–1¼ in (2–30 mm)	Damsel & Dragonflies ½–2 in (10–50 mm)
JANUARY	■			
FEBRUARY	■			
MARCH	■			
APRIL	■		■	
MAY	■	■	■	■
JUNE	■	■	■	■
JULY	■	■	■	■
AUGUST	■	■	■	■
SEPTEMBER	■	■	■	
OCTOBER	■			
NOVEMBER	■			
DECEMBER	■			

SUGGESTED ARTIFICIALS:
(Some flies are effective for multiple naturals.)

Midges	Caddis	Mayflies	Damsel & Dragonflies
San Juan Worm	Stick Fly	GE Nymph	Distressed Damsel
Bead Head Brassie	Silver Invicta	Troth Pheasant Tail	Troth Pheasant Tail
Tube Buzzer	Red Palmer	Sparkle Gulper	Green Butt Tadpole (Olive)
Barden's Hare's Ear	Grousewing	Duck's Dun	Olive Bumble
Diawl Bach	Moser Caddis Pupa	Greenwell's Glory	Olive Dabbler
Bibio	Fiery Brown	Glitter Spinner	
	Sparkle Gnat		

Light activity – sporadic feeding
Increased activity – regular feeding
Heavy activity – heavy feeding
Intense activity – intense preoccupied feeding

Crustaceans $1/4$–$3/4$ in (5–15 mm)	Corixa $1/4$–$1/2$ in (5–10 mm)	Fish $3/4$–3 in (20–80 mm)	Terrestrials $1/4$–$1\,1/2$ in (5–40 mm)	Daphnia $1/16$–$1/4$ in (2–5 mm)	Snails $1/2$–$3/4$ in (10–20 mm)
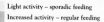					
Red Spot Shrimp	Barden's Hare's Ear	Minky	McMurray Ant	Red Arsed Wickham	Bibio
Killer Bug	Silver Invicta	Silver Invicta	Ethafoam Beetle	Dunkeld	Black Pennell
Hare's Ear (Flashback)		Hare's Ear (Flashback)	Halford Black Gnat	Green Butt Tadpole (Orange)	Ethafoam Beetle
Troth Pheasant Tail		Mason's Pheasant Tail	Dave's Hopper		
		Flat Roach	Coch-y-bondhu		
		Mini Appetizer			

STILLWATER SUNK

GENERALLY, TROUT PREFER to feed subsurface. In order to be effective when fishing stillwater, we have little option but to plunge down through the depths after them. Care at this point is essential, since not all fish will be dining in the deep. Be methodical in your approach. Think about the most likely depth, select the pattern, line, and leader that best serves your purpose and position below the surface, and move it in a way that emulates subsurface life and is guaranteed to appeal to trout.

Std 10–16

Bead Head Brassie
A personal variation on a theme, this fly has accounted for many midge feeders when fished on a floating line and long leader or used as a clear stalking pattern.

Std 10–16

Tube Buzzer
This makes a good close-copy midge pupa. Use either singularly, or as a dropper to a team on a floating line and long leader from the bank or sunk line from a boat.

Std 10–18

Suspender Para Midge
This self-buoyant pattern is perfect in a midge hatch when trout are harvesting the surface layers yet refuse a dry fly. Fish on fine tippets, singularly, to observed feeders.

Std & Ls 8–14

Stick Fly
This superb all-purpose reservoir pattern is best fished in conjunction with a floating line, long leader, and very slow retrieves.

Std 10–16

Lurex Spider
Good at all depths and speeds of retrieve, but best on a floating line, using a figure-eight retrieve or long, slow pulls.

Std & Ls 10–14

Montana
Leaded or not, fished fast or slow, near the surface or the bottom, this pattern is likely to get a response. This version has a fluorescent thorax.

Std 10–12

Barden's Hare's Ear
One of a range of deadly,
ultrasparse, "anorexic"
nymph designs by Bob
Barden, these patterns
can be devastating in a
variety of stillwater
scenarios.

Std 10–14

Mason's Pheasant Tail
The honey-colored tail
and beard hackle make this
a good general pattern.
Best fished at the point or
middle-dropper position
when boat fishing, using
a Wet Cel 3 format.

Std 10–16

Diawl Bach
The Welsh name means
"Little Devil." It is fished
during the height of midge
hatches at dawn or dusk.
Always fish this simple
but deadly fly on an
ultraslow retrieve.

Std & Ls 8–12

Green Butt Tadpole
Though not a purist's fly, this
is a particular favorite of
mine. In black or white, it is
all you need at the beginning
of the season.

Std 8–10

Mini Appetizer
This pattern excels
when fry are on the
menu. Can be fished
either on a floating or
sunk line.

Std 8–12

Distressed Damsel
This pattern is designed
to imitate the natural's
wiggle via the long tail,
while offering realism at
the thorax.

Std 8–12

Bewick's Booby
A fly from Queen Mother Reservoir,
near London. Fish with a very fast-
sinking line, short leaders, and an
almost static figure-eight retrieve, with
lengthy periods between to allow the fly
to rise and fall across the lake floor.

Std 4–10

Minky
Also called the Mink Zonker,
this is an exceptionally good bank-
fisher's fly, especially during early
season and fry time. A floating line and
long leader combined with slow retrieves
achieve the highest success rate.

CLASSIC STILLWATER WET

THE PATTERNS DESIGNED by our forebears, still much in evidence today, remain very effective, and have provided the inspiration for many modern stillwater flies. These classic flies originated in the highlands of Scotland or the Irish lakes. Through the years, these concoctions of fur, leather, and tinsel have inveigled salmon, sea trout, brown trout, and rainbows alike. The patterns are usually fished in threes or fours to the front of a broad-sided, drifting boat, in a rhythmic method.

Std 8–16

Bibio

There can be few more famous flies for lake fishing than the Bibio. Use in hatches of dark to black midge or whenever a hint of color is called for.

Std 8–16

Irish Mallard & Claret

As well as an effective sea trout pattern for tea-stained water, this also makes a useful point fly, especially in the evening and on dark days.

Std 8–16

Wickham's Fancy

One of the truly great wet flies, perfect when caddis or red midge are active or as a general sea trout attractor. An essential point or middle-dropper pattern.

Std 8–16

Black Pennell

This turn-of-the-century pattern can be found in most fly boxes. Especially good during the early season as a point or middle-dropper when black midge are hatching.

Std 8–16

Silver Invicta

This classic wet fly is best used on lakes and ponds, either as the middle-dropper or tail position when short- or long-lining from a drifting boat using a floating line.

Std 8–16

Fiery Brown

As a wet-caddis design this pattern is excellent, as either a point or middle-dropper, especially from summer to autumn. It has also developed a reputation for sea trout.

Std 8–16

Red Palmer

This pattern is extremely useful in rolling waves and overcast conditions. It is fished fairly quickly in order to create a discernible wake.

Std 8–14

Clan Chief

An excellent top- or middle-dropper pattern, especially in tea-stained water. Suitable either for freshwater trout or sea-trout.

Std 8–16

Olive Bumble

This is probably the most popular of T. Kingsmill Moore's lake patterns. Essential in any drift angler's box, and superb as a topper in a big wave.

Std 8–16

Red Arsed Wickham

The fluorescent red tail makes this pattern highly visible both in low light or tea-stained water. Fished as a top-dropper on a floating line.

Std 8–16

Dunkeld

This pattern is a true classic for lake rainbows or browns. Best on the point or middle-dropper position, especially on bright days.

Std 6–14

Goat's Toe

This pattern sports a fluorescent red wool tail instead of the usual plain red. More a middle- or top-dropper fly.

Std 8–12

Dabbler

This fly has taken Ireland by storm in the past few years, fished either on the top- or middle-dropper. It is great in all but flat calm. Variations include olive, claret, fiery brown, and gold versions.

Std & Ls 4–14

Muddler Minnow

Dan Gappen from Michigan created this truly classic fly, and Tom Saville introduced it to British stillwater fly-fishing circles. A great small-fish pattern in large sizes, it is even better in small sizes for imitating hatching caddis.

STILLWATER SURFACE

O VER THE LAST ten years, fishing on the surface of lakes has
rapidly increased in popularity. New patterns, methods,
and techniques have burst upon the scene with bewildering
speed. However, fishing the dry fly, or damp, for that matter,
remains one of the most relaxing and simple methods. Accurate
casting, anticipation of the trout's next move or rise form, and a
reasonably gentle presentation with the correct pattern
and timing on the strike are the key elements.

Std 16–24

Black Midge

An autopsy of any trout
will reveal a quantity of
tiny black specks. This
pattern is an ideal imitator
of hatching Chironomids.
Fish singularly on
fine tipppets.

Std 10–14

Hare's Face Midge

The properties of the
Hare's Face are very
effective when fish are
feeding on midge.
This is one of my
favorites when trout
are rising in a
gentle wave.

Std 10–16

Bob's Bits

This pattern is a classic
that represents a wide
spectrum of trout food.
Fished static, it will often
encourage fish to rise.
Use a sinking compound
such as mud so that your
leader tippet submerges.

Std 10–16

Shipman's Buzzer

Dave Shipman's fly
suggests a midge emerging
or hatching on the
surface. This fly should
be "ginked" to float and
fished either static or slow
in a figure eight.

Std 10–14

Grafham Hopper

Fished static and cast
accurately, even at
short range, this single
fly has accounted for
legions of trout. The
body may be orange,
olive, or claret.

Std 16–24

Halo Emerger

Based on Gary
LaFontaine's pattern, this
design is aimed at midge-
eating surface feeders.
Fish singularly on a
12–15 ft (4–5 m)
leader to 5 or 7x tippet.

Std 12–16

Greenwell's Glory
*This dry version of
Canon Greenwell's
classic wet fly remains
one of the best stillwater
olive patterns, and is
mandatory in reservoir
anglers' boxes.*

Std 14–18

Grousewing
*This pattern imitates the
summer hordes of caddis
of the same name. Fish it
static or gently tweaked,
singularly or in a team.
At its best when fished
in the evening.*

Std 16–22

Para Midge
*A specially designed midge
pattern for selective trout
feeding on the surface.
Vary the chenille's color
to offer a full range. Fish
on a 12–15 ft (4–5 m)
leader to 5 or 7x tippet.*

Std 14–18

Sparkle Gulper
*Trout can get very
difficult in evening flat
calms. This low-riding
pattern is effective in both
midge or olive hatches.
Fish singularly on a
long leader.*

Std 14–22

Sparkle Gnat
*Fish this pattern either
singularly on a long
leader, or three at a time
when boat fishing in
gentle ripples. The
twinkle tail suggests a
discarded nymph shuck.*

Std 10–14

JC Emerger
*This semidry general
attractor should be fished
awash in the surface film,
singularly or in threes from
boat or bank. Have your
leader tippet well
degreased prior to casting.*

Ls 4–12

Flat Roach
*Probably the most lethal dead or dying
fish imitation available. Although
troublesome to tie, it is well worth the
effort. Fish static on a floating line in and
around fry activity or weed beds. A
twitch can often initiate a response.*

Std 8–12

Lively Mayfly
*By chance I picked up a book by
Chauncy Lively in the Fly-Fishers'
Club, and by adapting one of his
patterns evolved this fly. It enjoys
considerable success, and remains my
most successful dry-dun pattern.*

MIGRATORY TACTICS

WHEN SEA-RUNNING fish enter fresh water, their behavior varies from species to species. However, all fish have some habits in common, and this will help you to devise your tactics. Most fish stop to rest, and some prefishing detective work will enable you to discover their resting places and to concentrate your efforts in these areas. It is wise to use the services of a gillie or guide if time is short. As they live locally and fish the waters on a daily basis, their knowledge can eliminate a great deal of fruitless effort.

KEY TO SUCCESS

Look out for current deflections, such as fallen logs or midstream boulders. Pools are invariably holding areas, where the deep "belly" of the pool is used by day, the faster "tail" in low light. Head for the more oxygenated areas of low water. Remember – look, analyze, then fish.

Hold as much line as possible off water to allow fly to sink deeper

Cast downstream and across on a slack line

Take a pace or two downstream after each cast to slow fly's drift and fish fresh water

▼ **Downstream Fishing**
Depth and fly size is the key, especially in the case of salmon. In water temperatures above 50°F (10°C), a smaller fly is usually the best choice. When the water is warmer than the air, a big fly is usually better. For sluggish to medium currents choose a floating or sinking tip line, for medium to fast a sinking tip or intermediate, and for fast flows a sunk line.

MENDING LINE

When fishing downstream methods, you will often find that your pattern skates too fast across the current. You are left with two alternatives – change your line, or make an upstream mend that will delay the fly's sweep across the flow. Mending should become second nature. As the fly line initially alights on the surface it is quickly rolled upstream to form a belly. You will find that it is far easier to do this operation with double-tapered line rather than with weight-forward.

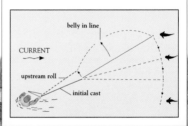

belly in line

CURRENT

upstream roll

initial cast

Mend line as necessary to slow fly's drift

Quarter river in a series of sweeping arcs

Work bucktails and streamers with rod tip to imitate small bait fish

MIGRATORY TACTICS (Continued)

DEEP WADING

Altering your position relative to that of the quarry, either from the bank, or by wading out, allows you to swing the fly through the taking area with more variety of speed, depth, and angle. The midstream position allows you to hold the fly longer in the taking area.

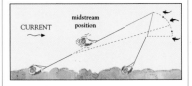

CURRENT

midstream position

KEY TO SUCCESS

Tenacity is the key with sea-running species. Constantly vary your approach, line angle, and fly pattern. Try hand-lining (backing up) the pattern across the stream in slack water. In low water, fish the oxygenated areas around boulders and the throats and tails of pools. During hot, bright spells, fish in the cool early morning or late evening.

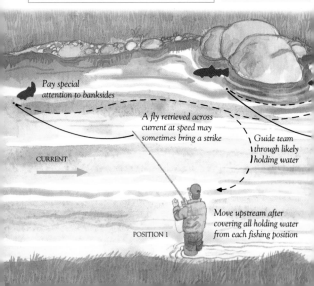

Pay special attention to banksides

A fly retrieved across current at speed may sometimes bring a strike

Guide team through likely holding water

CURRENT

Move upstream after covering all holding water from each fishing position

POSITION 1

▶ **Atlantic Salmon**
The ultimate prize for most anglers, this magnificent salmon has been "tailed" by the captor rather than landed by net. This is done by playing the salmon into slack, shallow water, then wading out so that the quarry is between you and the bank. By keeping the line under tension it is possible to stoop down and grasp the fish by the fleshy "wrist" just before the tail.

▼ **Upstream Fishing**
When tackling migratory fish that are normally approached by the across-and-down technique, an upstream style may also work, especially for sea trout and steelhead. Remember, with migratory species, it is important to continually present your fly in a different manner.

Pay special attention to eddies and reverse currents

At end of drift, retrieve with a steady figure eight or small twitches

Cast upstream and across and allow flies to fish back down at current's speed

POSITION 2

MIGRATORY ATTRACTORS

Arguments still rage as to whether fish coming from the salt do in fact feed in fresh water. The consensus seems to be a guarded "probably," especially in the case of char and trout. Nevertheless, nonspecific patterns tend to be the first choice, with the emphasis on size, as influenced by time of day, height of water, and air and water temperature. As so many variances apply in this branch of sport, seeking local knowledge is vital. However, the following forms are a reliable selection.

Std 6–12

Egg Fly

Universally popular with fly fishers in the US as an imitation of roe. Fish this pattern hard on the river bed using a sinking tip line and dead-drift tactics over spawning areas and other gravelly runs.

Std 4–14

Teeny Nymph

This simple fly, fashioned from pheasant by Jim Teeny, forms the mainstay of his armory and has caught most game fish, including Atlantic salmon. An indispensable pattern.

Ls 6–14

Medicine (Mallard)

This deadly blue-and-silver pattern was developed by Hugh Falkus. It is a river fly and an ideal all-purpose pattern, suiting most conditions either on a sunk or floating line.

Std 6–14

Zulu

The definitive loch-style fly for darker days. A top- or middle-dropper, or even the point fly. A catcher of trout and sea trout throughout the British Isles.

Std 4–12

Umpqua Special

This 1935 pattern, attributed to Don Hunter, originated on Oregon's Umpqua River. Patterns developed for particular rivers are usually effective.

Std 4–12

Silver Rat

A wonderfully adaptable pattern, forming part of a series created for the salmon-rich waters of Quebec. This pattern works in all sizes, river heights, and seasons.

Ls 4–12

Ferry Canyon

This Randall Kaufmann fly emphasizes how steelhead patterns have altered dramatically by incorporating new materials and colors. Purple has become extremely popular for dark days and evening use.

Std 4–10

General Practitioner

This pattern is still one of the finest "prawn" dressings available. Devised by Esmond Drury, many salmon fishers see this pattern, in various sizes, as their first line of attack. It is effective in all conditions.

Std 4–12

Bomber (Finland)

Originated in Lapland and used for Atlantic salmon on the Tana River, this pattern is also used as a trout fly during the summer, when large caddis hatch. Also useful in autumn for steelheads.

Std 4–12

Ally's Shrimp

A lighter, more mobile variation on the prawn theme than the General Practitioner. This all-season, all-water pattern by Alistair Gowans has become a classic in a remarkably short time.

Std 2–8

Flash Fly

Though primarily an Alaskan-silver and king-salmon fly for colored water, patterns such as this are a boon even though they resemble a spinner. Best fished from near to the bottom up to midwater.

Ls & Std 2–14

Willie Gunn

This is the ultimate early or late high-water pattern. In either its Waddington or tube form, as shown here, it is deadly. Named by the famous gillie, Willie Gunn, it echoes the autumnal colors effective for late- or early-running fish.

MAINTENANCE

"LOOK AFTER YOUR tackle and it will look after you" should be indelibly printed on your mind; mud, grit, sand, and general lack of care can cost you money and may occasionally lose fish. A few moments spent bathing a line in a lukewarm, mildly soapy water will not only extend the line's life, but enable you to cast farther and achieve optimum performance. Similarly, cleaning the rod blank, handles, and reel seats, checking nets for holes and waders for leaks, and caring for your tackle box takes very little time, but it enhances your enjoyment and helps to achieve better results.

SIDE VIEW

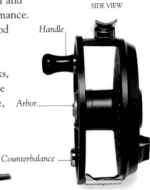

Handle

Arbor

Counterbalance

FRONT VIEW

The Fly Reel
A fly reel is a delicate precision instrument. It needs to be oiled, cleaned, and cared for because you will be relying on its smooth running and trouble-free checking system to help you land the quarry.

Preset drag dial to balance spool and tippet strength

ROD CARE

Look for chinks in the varnish, and mud and grit in the ring areas and reel seat. Pay special attention if you have hit the rod blank or a rod with a leaded fly, knocked against a gunwhale, or dropped your rod on the rocks. Always clean and dry your rod after use.

Cork Handles
With use your cork handle will deteriorate. If holes appear, or just small areas need attention, a quick application of plastic wood-filler will plug any gaps.

Worn Rings
Worn rings are ruinous to fly lines and should be professionally replaced. If ignored, they can not only cause damage to lines but also hamper presentation.

WORN LINES

A fly-line should be regularly checked for wear at the junction of the leader and line (A) and if necessary retied. Also look for serrations and abrasions (B), severe cracking (C), and miniature surface cracks that attract dirt (D). Lines with these faults should be replaced.

A

B

C

D

INTERNAL WORKINGS

Ratchet checking mechanism

Disk-brake checking mechanism

Checking Mechanisms
Pay particular attention to the checking systems. Grit or sand can ruin a mechanism in surprisingly few revolutions. Periodically wash the reel in warm soapy water and oil regularly.

First Aid

WATER IS A HAZARD; a recent graze or open cut is always at risk of infection as water has a nasty habit of exacerbating the problem. A quick dab of antiseptic, having first cleaned the area, should be considered mandatory practice. Take sensible precautions, protect skin from intense sun, protect eyes from wayward hooks and casts with glasses, watch out for blisters, and wear appropriate clothing. Also, keep some form of basic first-aid kit handy. These are freely available from medical and some fishing outlets. But remember, if in doubt, always seek proper medical guidance.

Removing a Hook

It is very common for a hook to become impaled in the skin. Firstly, don't panic. If it is in a fleshy part of the hand, you will find it relatively easy to remove. If the hook is very deep, however, or anywhere near delicate parts, such as your face, seek medical help.

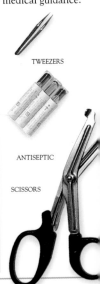

TWEEZERS

ANTISEPTIC

SCISSORS

1 If the hook is in just past the barb, loop about 30 cm (12 in) of strong nylon around the bend of the hook.

2 Pressing down on the shank of the fly opens the entrance wound. Grasp the nylon strands in your free hand and pull quickly.

THE BASIC FIRST-AID KIT

In reality you need very little for an
effective precautionary kit. Stick to
items you are confident about using.
An antiseptic of some sort is essential.
Cotton wool, tweezers, plasters, sun
block, and scissors are all valuable.
Painkillers can sometimes be useful
but follow the guidelines.

HOSTILE ENVIRONMENTS

*The clothes you carry can be
important to survival. Always
make sure you are dressed
appropriately for the terrain and
conditions in which you are
fishing. Bad weather can
descend at any time. By using a
modern lightweight layering
system you will be able to add or
subtract garments as necessary.*

SUN BLOCK

BANDAGES

SAFETY PINS

FIRST-AID BAG

PLASTERS

KEEPING A RECORD
of your CATCH

A DAY'S FISHING, a specific catch, or
a notable area or fly can all slip
away like mist in the morning if some
form of record is not kept. Looking back
over past days by the water can form the
very foundation of a new approach; an empathy with a certain
water can blossom. Fly patterns and insect emergence
can be dovetailed into specific periods. And if that
is not enough, a huge amount of pleasure can be
gained from reliving past encounters and epic
battles. Even recording abject failure can provide
useful information, if only as a reminder not to do
the same thing again!

You will find out for yourself which information is most
relevant to your style of fishing. For the salmon fisher, it will
probably be the air and water temperature; for the stillwater
fisher, weather, wind, and water will be the most pertinent.
A few minutes is all it takes
to record priceless
information for
your future
enjoyment
and benefit.

DATE

TIME *from*   *to*

PLACE

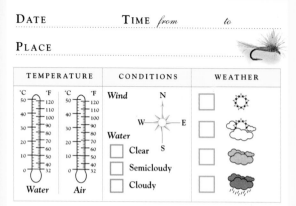

TEMPERATURE	CONDITIONS	WEATHER

FLY USED	SPECIES	WEIGHT	LENGTH

NOTES

DATE   TIME *from*   *to*

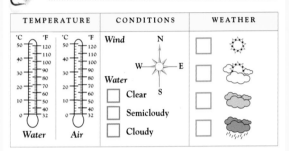

PLACE

TEMPERATURE	CONDITIONS	WEATHER
°C °F °C °F 50–120 50–120 40–110 40–110 100 100 30–90 30–90 20–70 20–70 60 60 10–50 10–50 40 40 0–32 0–32 *Water* *Air*	*Wind* N W E S *Water* ☐ Clear ☐ Semicloudy ☐ Cloudy	☐ ☐ ☐ ☐

FLY USED	SPECIES	WEIGHT	LENGTH

NOTES

DATE _____ **TIME** *from* _____ *to* _____

PLACE _____

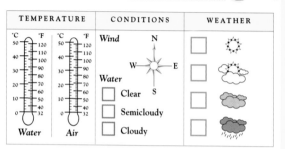

TEMPERATURE	CONDITIONS	WEATHER

Temperature:

°C / °F (Water) — 50/120, 40/110, 40/100, 30/90, 30/80, 20/70, 20/60, 10/50, 10/40, 0/32

°C / °F (Air) — 50/120, 40/110, 40/100, 30/90, 30/80, 20/70, 20/60, 10/50, 10/40, 0/32

Water   Air

Conditions:

Wind   N   W   E   S

Water
☐ Clear
☐ Semicloudy
☐ Cloudy

Weather: ☐ ☐ ☐ ☐

FLY USED	SPECIES	WEIGHT	LENGTH

NOTES

_____
_____
_____

DATE .... TIME *from* .... *to* ....

 PLACE ....

TEMPERATURE	CONDITIONS	WEATHER

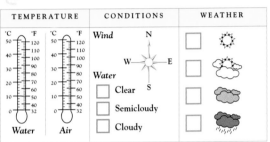

FLY USED	SPECIES	WEIGHT	LENGTH

NOTES

....

....

....

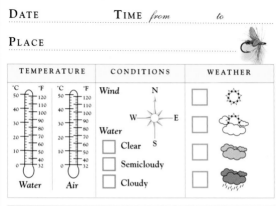

DATE		TIME *from*		*to*	

PLACE

TEMPERATURE	CONDITIONS	WEATHER

FLY USED	SPECIES	WEIGHT	LENGTH

NOTES

DATE .... TIME *from* .... *to* ....

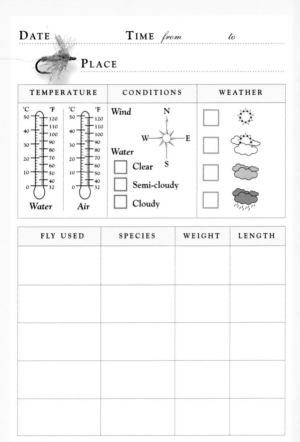

PLACE ....

TEMPERATURE	CONDITIONS	WEATHER

TEMPERATURE

°C   °F   °C   °F
50 — 120   50 — 120
       — 110   — 110
40 — 100   40 — 100
       — 90   — 90
30 — 80   30 — 80
       — 70   — 70
20 — 60   20 — 60
       — 50   — 50
10 — 40   10 — 40
0 — 32   0 — 32

Water   Air

CONDITIONS

Wind   N

W ——☀—— E

Water   S

☐ Clear
☐ Semi-cloudy
☐ Cloudy

WEATHER

☐
☐
☐
☐

FLY USED	SPECIES	WEIGHT	LENGTH

NOTES
....
....
....

TEMPERATURE	CONDITIONS	WEATHER

TEMPERATURE:
°C °F °C °F
50 — 120   50 — 120
— 110   — 110
40 — 100   40 — 100
— 90   — 90
30 — 80   30 — 80
— 70   — 70
20 — 60   20 — 60
10 — 50   10 — 50
— 40   — 40
0 — 32   0 — 32

Water   Air

CONDITIONS:
Wind

N
W — E
S

Water
☐ Clear
☐ Semi-cloudy
☐ Cloudy

WEATHER:
☐
☐
☐
☐

FLY USED	SPECIES	WEIGHT	LENGTH

NOTES
....
....
....

DATE .... TIME *from* .... *to* ....

PLACE ....

TEMPERATURE	CONDITIONS	WEATHER

TEMPERATURE

°C   °F   °C   °F
50 —— 120   50 —— 120
40 —— 110   40 —— 110
   —— 100   —— 100
30 —— 90   30 —— 90
   —— 80   —— 80
20 —— 70   20 —— 70
   —— 60   —— 60
10 —— 50   10 —— 50
   —— 40   —— 40
0 —— 32   0 —— 32

Water   **Air**

CONDITIONS

Wind   N

W ——☀—— E

Water   S

☐ Clear

☐ Semicloudy

☐ Cloudy

WEATHER

☐

☐

☐

☐

FLY USED	SPECIES	WEIGHT	LENGTH

NOTES ....

....

....

DATE

TIME *from*   *to*

PLACE

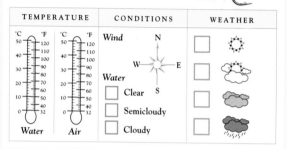

TEMPERATURE	CONDITIONS	WEATHER

Wind

N

W — E

S

Water

☐ Clear

☐ Semicloudy

☐ Cloudy

Water   Air

☐ ☐ ☐ ☐

FLY USED	SPECIES	WEIGHT	LENGTH

NOTES

....

....

....

PLACE ....

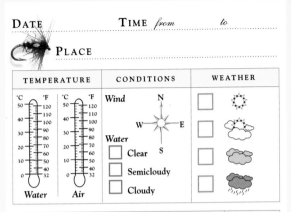

FLY USED	SPECIES	WEIGHT	LENGTH

NOTES ....

....

....

PLACE ....

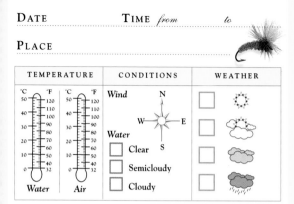

TEMPERATURE	CONDITIONS	WEATHER

FLY USED	SPECIES	WEIGHT	LENGTH

NOTES

....

....

....

DATE .... TIME *from* .... *to* ....

PLACE ....

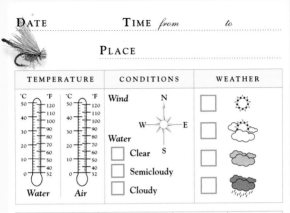

TEMPERATURE	CONDITIONS	WEATHER

Water / Air

Wind

N
W — E
S

Water
☐ Clear
☐ Semicloudy
☐ Cloudy

FLY USED	SPECIES	WEIGHT	LENGTH

NOTES ....
....
....

DATE .... **TIME** *from* .... *to* ....

PLACE ....

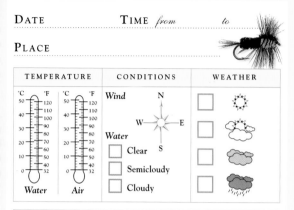

TEMPERATURE	CONDITIONS	WEATHER
Water / Air	Wind	
	Water □ Clear □ Semicloudy □ Cloudy	

FLY USED	SPECIES	WEIGHT	LENGTH

NOTES ....
....
....

DATE .... TIME *from* .... *to* ....

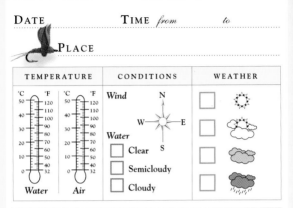

PLACE ....

TEMPERATURE	CONDITIONS	WEATHER

Wind

N

W ——✲—— E

S

Water

☐ Clear

☐ Semicloudy

☐ Cloudy

FLY USED	SPECIES	WEIGHT	LENGTH

NOTES ....

....

....

DATE .... TIME *from* .... *to* ....

PLACE ....

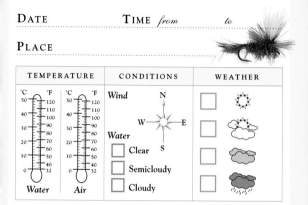

TEMPERATURE	CONDITIONS	WEATHER

FLY USED	SPECIES	WEIGHT	LENGTH

NOTES
....
....
....

DATE .... TIME *from* .... *to* ....

PLACE ....

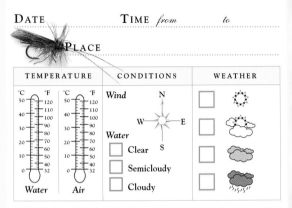

TEMPERATURE	CONDITIONS	WEATHER

Wind

Water

☐ Clear

☐ Semicloudy

☐ Cloudy

FLY USED	SPECIES	WEIGHT	LENGTH

NOTES

....

....

....

DATE

TIME *from*   *to*

PLACE

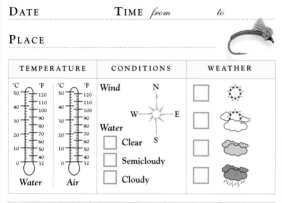

TEMPERATURE	CONDITIONS	WEATHER

TEMPERATURE

°C   °F   °C   °F
50 — 120   50 — 120
40 — 110   40 — 110
   — 100   — 100
30 — 90   30 — 90
   — 80   — 80
20 — 70   20 — 70
   — 60   — 60
10 — 50   10 — 50
   — 40   — 40
 0 — 32   0 — 32

Water   *Air*

CONDITIONS

Wind   N

W ——☀—— E

Water   S

☐ Clear

☐ Semicloudy

☐ Cloudy

WEATHER

☐

☐

☐

☐

FLY USED	SPECIES	WEIGHT	LENGTH

NOTES

....

....

....

DATE .... **TIME** *from* .... *to* ....

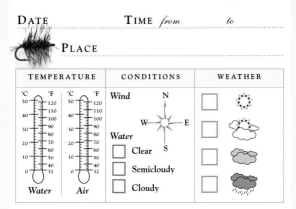

PLACE ....

TEMPERATURE	CONDITIONS	WEATHER

FLY USED	SPECIES	WEIGHT	LENGTH

NOTES ....

....

....

....

DATE .... **TIME** *from* .... *to* ....

PLACE ....

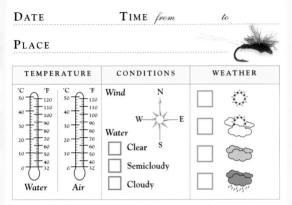

TEMPERATURE	CONDITIONS	WEATHER

Wind

Water — Air

Water
- Clear
- Semicloudy
- Cloudy

FLY USED	SPECIES	WEIGHT	LENGTH

NOTES ....
....
....

PLACE

TEMPERATURE	CONDITIONS	WEATHER

TEMPERATURE

°C °F   °C °F
50 — 120   50 — 120
40 — 110   40 — 110
    100   100
30 — 90   30 — 90
20 — 80   20 — 80
    70   70
10 — 60   10 — 60
    50   50
0 — 40   0 — 40
    32   32

Water   *Air*

CONDITIONS

Wind   N

W — E

S

Water

☐ Clear

☐ Semicloudy

☐ Cloudy

WEATHER

☐
☐
☐
☐

FLY USED	SPECIES	WEIGHT	LENGTH

NOTES

....
....
....

| DATE | | TIME *from* | | *to* | |

PLACE

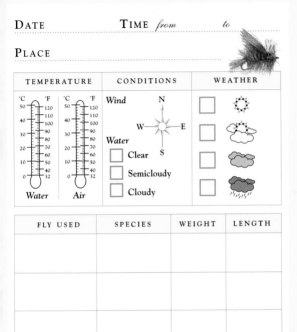

| TEMPERATURE | | CONDITIONS | WEATHER |

TEMPERATURE

°C °F
50 120
40 110
    100
30 90
    80
20 70
    60
10 50
    40
0   32

Water

°C °F
50 120
40 110
    100
30 90
    80
20 70
    60
10 50
    40
0   32

Air

CONDITIONS

Wind   N

W ——☀—— E

Water   S

☐ Clear

☐ Semicloudy

☐ Cloudy

WEATHER

☐

☐

☐

☐

FLY USED	SPECIES	WEIGHT	LENGTH

NOTES

DATE .... TIME *from* .... *to* ....

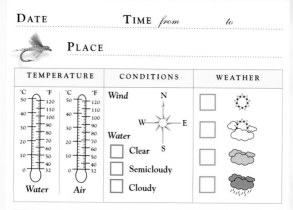

PLACE ....

TEMPERATURE	CONDITIONS	WEATHER

Water **Air**

Wind

N

W · E

S

Water

☐ Clear

☐ Semicloudy

☐ Cloudy

FLY USED	SPECIES	WEIGHT	LENGTH

NOTES

....

....

....

DATE .... **TIME** *from* .... *to* ....

PLACE ....

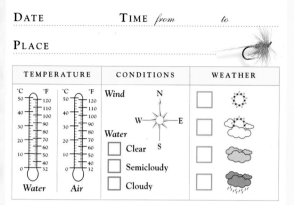

TEMPERATURE	CONDITIONS	WEATHER
°C °F °C °F	*Wind* N	
Water Air	W E	
	Water S	
	☐ Clear	
	☐ Semicloudy	
	☐ Cloudy	

FLY USED	SPECIES	WEIGHT	LENGTH

NOTES ....
....
....

DATE .... TIME *from* .... *to* ....

PLACE ....

TEMPERATURE	CONDITIONS	WEATHER

TEMPERATURE

°C / °F
50 — 120
40 — 110
   — 100
30 — 90
   — 80
20 — 70
   — 60
10 — 50
   — 40
0 — 32

Water

°C / °F
50 — 120
40 — 110
   — 100
30 — 90
   — 80
20 — 70
   — 60
10 — 50
   — 40
0 — 32

Air

CONDITIONS

Wind

N
W — E
S

Water
☐ Clear
☐ Semicloudy
☐ Cloudy

WEATHER

☐
☐
☐
☐

FLY USED	SPECIES	WEIGHT	LENGTH

NOTES
....
....
....

DATE   TIME *from*   *to*

PLACE

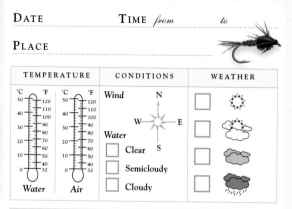

TEMPERATURE	CONDITIONS	WEATHER
°C °F °C °F 50 120 50 120 40 110 40 110 100 100 30 90 30 90 80 80 20 70 20 70 60 60 10 50 10 50 40 40 0 32 0 32 **Water** **Air**	*Wind* N W E S *Water* ☐ Clear ☐ Semicloudy ☐ Cloudy	☐ ☐ ☐ ☐

FLY USED	SPECIES	WEIGHT	LENGTH

NOTES
....
....
....

ACKNOWLEDGMENTS

I would like to offer my deep, personal thanks to the people and companies that made various sections of this book possible. Marc Bale & Gerry Siem at *Sage*, Brian Frittell & Andrew Witkowski at *Farlow's*, Robin Gow, Jim Hadderell & Barry Welham at *Orvis*, Anne & Philip Parkinson at *Sportfish*, Bill Klien at *Patagonia*, *House of Hardy*, Chris Leibrandt at *Ryobi Masterline*, Bruce Richards at *3M*, Nigel Jackson & Neil at *Dever Springs Lake*, Garry Coxon, and Jeff Allum.

I would also like to thank David Lamb, Frank Ritter, and Derek Coombes at Dorling Kindersley for their huge contribution to this project and Arthur Brown and Alistair Plumb at Cooling Brown who got everything into tangible form and made it fun. Finally, and by no means least, Carole, Annabelle, and Alex, my long-suffering family. Oh, and I nearly forgot, the trout and salmon we pursue to the far corners of the globe. May they swim forever and tease us to distraction. I dedicate this little book to their continued survival and magnificence.

Dorling Kindersley and Cooling Brown would also like to thank the following people for their part in this project: Annabel Morgan, Constance M. Robinson, Clive Graham-Ranger, and James Harrison for their editorial assistance; Andy Crawford, Gary Ombler and Steve Gorton for additional photography.

PICTURE CREDITS

Kevin Cullimore: 2, 15tr; Peter Cockwill: 16; Peter Gathercole: 5r, 6b, 7, 8, 9, 13t, 14t, 14b, 18, 20, 24, 25, 27t, 27bl, 27br, 28b, 29tl, 29bl, 29br, 30b, 31tl, 30tr, 30bl, 32b, 33t, 33c, 33br, 34b, 35tl, 35cl, 55, 59, 69, 80; Charles Jardine: 13c, 17t, 46t, 47, 48t, 52r, 53t, 67, 77, 79, 81, 95; Bill McMillan: 19t; Stephen Oliver: 12; Oxford Scientific: 26b (Colin Milkins), 29tr (David Wright), 34tr (Peter Parkes), 35tr (Peter O'Toole), 35cl (Barry Watts); Marty Sherman: 21tr, 22, 23tl, 23c
Abbreviations: t = top; b = bottom; c = center; l = left; r = right

Illustrations by Charles Jardine, Ian Heard, and Clive Spong